DESIGNING AND DECORATING
A PERIOD DOLLS' HOUSE

HIGH STREET

44
MORNINGTON
HOUSE

Rebecca Micallef

DESIGNING AND DECORATING
A PERIOD DOLLS' HOUSE

THE CROWOOD PRESS

CONTENTS

Introduction 6

1 Choosing a Dolls' House 8

2 Getting Started on the Dolls' House 21

3 The Dolls' House Exterior 30

4 The Dolls' House Interior 50

5 Lighting the Dolls' House 63

6 Staircases 75

7 Furnishing the Dolls' House 82

8 Accessories for the Dolls' House 114

9 Completing the Dolls' House 133

Templates 139

List of Suppliers 141

Index 142

INTRODUCTION

The world of dolls' houses is one of the largest and most sought-after hobbies around the globe, going back thousands of years. The oldest examples of dolls' houses were discovered in the Egyptian pyramids, and dated from at least five thousand years ago; they were used for religious purposes.

In the sixteenth century dolls' houses were introduced into European countries. They were mostly known as 'baby houses', and were so called

Dolls' house cabinet of Petronella Dunois c. 1676, displayed at the Rijksmuseum in Amsterdam.

because at that time, dolls were referred to as 'babies'. Another reason was that some were replicas of the bigger house that the owners lived in. Each house was uniquely built by skilled craftsmen, and decorated to the smallest detail, as might be found in any typical rich and noble household of that time. None of these treasures were intended for children to play with, but were displayed with pride to show the social status and wealth of the owners. The first recorded aristocrats and noble families to have these 'baby houses' lived in Germany, the Netherlands and England.

In the seventeenth and eighteenth centuries, dolls' houses were also used for educational purposes, for young girls to learn how to run a household with servants. In the Netherlands, dolls' houses were built a little differently and were called 'Dutch cabinet houses'. Each room within the cabinet was highly decorated with beautiful wallpaper, delicate furniture pieces and expensive miniatures.

In the Victorian era dolls' houses became quite a tradition amongst middle-class families. The dolls, miniature china, accessories and wooden furniture became more affordable. By then the dolls' house was also introduced to smaller children as a plaything, and found a prominent place in the nursery.

After World War II, dolls' houses increased in popularity and also in production in European countries and America. Factories started to mass produce them and their miniatures, consequently with less detail, and they were sold commercially

An original Triang dolls' house, Model No. 76, from the 1950s.

for children at a much more affordable price. This continued to the present day, when both collectors and children enjoy their own versions of dolls' houses.

This book is written for those wanting to venture into this amazing hobby, and is intended as a step-by-step guide to building your own dolls' house, and decorating both the exterior and the interior.

Part of the dolls' house collection at My Miniature World.

CHAPTER 1

CHOOSING A DOLLS' HOUSE

Choosing a dolls' house is very exciting, especially if it is for the very first time. Some will go for their dream dolls' house, some will look for one similar to the dolls' house they owned during their childhood, while others have no idea at all what they want.

Choosing a dolls' house is not always easy, especially for those who don't know where to begin. A few aspects should be considered before any commitment is made to the work involved. Unfortunately this is a common mistake made by most newcomers to the hobby, who will often give up on the project at the very beginning.

There are a few options when it comes to constructing a dolls' house. Most beginners would prefer to purchase a dolls' house kit, as they consider this easier, and they can make their own modifications to the kit. Others want to design and build their own dolls' house, and I can guarantee that this is not as difficult as some might think, even for a beginner. The possibilities for this method are endless. A few room boxes of the same size can easily be put one against another or stacked on top of each other, making a perfectly acceptable dolls' house.

SIZE

The size and details of the project play a significant role when choosing a dolls' house. Dolls' houses come in different shapes and sizes, so the first thing to consider is where it is to be positioned; then take measurements of the area, and consider the surface or the piece of furniture where the finished project will be placed. This will give a clear picture of how big it should be. Sometimes it is surprising how large a dolls' house can be, even if you might imagine it would have to be much smaller.

An example of a dolls' house built with three room boxes.

An example of the exterior of a dolls' house.

A two-roomed dolls' house, ideal for a beginner.

When purchasing a dolls' house kit, always check the measurements of the finished building, either from the shop dealer, or as provided on the packaging. For a beginner I would suggest a four- to six-roomed dolls' house as it is easier to handle and can be quite straightforward. A few beginners might only be interested in getting one huge twelve-roomed dolls' house, but they might be better advised to try out a one-room box or a two-roomed dolls' house before taking on a much bigger challenge. This will help to boost confidence and experience, it will give the builder a chance to learn from their own mistakes, and will give a better idea of what is involved in building a dolls' house.

STYLE AND PERIOD

Like any normal house, dolls' houses come in various styles and periods, and this is one of the most important factors to consider when planning to build a dolls' house. You might prefer a period dolls' house, which can be built in a particular era and time frame – though in this case make sure to keep to the period features, and never combine two different period styles unless the house is of a much later period, when a few earlier styled pieces can be added to the project. The décor of the exterior and interior of the house should be considered, as also the colour scheme and patterns, and the lighting, furniture and accessories that were used in that particular time.

If you are not sure of the details of a particular era, it is always best to do some historical research. The following is a guide to the different historical periods and the styles that distinguish them, hopefully making it easier for you to decide which you will prefer to work with.

Tudor (1485–1603)
Tudor is one of the oldest styles in dolls' houses, going back to the time of King Henry VII and

Tudor style: medieval living quarters.

Queen Elizabeth I. Much of it is known as medieval, together with Renaissance and Gothic. Tudor-style houses are distinguished by their half-timbered buildings and their steeply pitched gable roofs, the decorative masonry of the chimneys and the leaded windows.

Georgian (1714–1830)

The Georgian style is typified by the terraced house dating back to the reigns of kings George I, George II, George III and George IV. A classical Georgian house was built in brick in a rectangular or square shape, with symmetrical windows and shutters. Baroque details might also be noticed in grand entrances, with columns, arches and high ceilings embellished with pediments and decorative mouldings.

Regency (1811–1820)

The Regency era goes back to the early nineteenth century when King George IV was Prince Regent. Even though it is considered part of the late Georgian period, the Regency style mostly applies to the interior design, and the way the rooms were highly decorated in a neoclassical style. Regency-style houses were typically decorated with vertically striped wallpaper, and furnished with elegant furniture and the fine arts of the period.

A Georgian style little girl's bedroom.

An example of a Regency style drawing room.

Victorian (1837–1901)

'Victorian' refers to Queen Victoria's reign, however, many factors in architecture and décor that are termed as 'Victorian style' became popular much later during Queen Victoria's era, from around the 1850s during the Industrial Revolution. During this period wealth increased and families could afford to live in a three-storey terraced house with steeply pitched roofs, painted brick walls, ornate gables and painted iron railings. Rooftops were finished off with church-like finials and octagonal or round towers and turrets. Bay windows and porches were quite popular, and a few houses also had a small garden. Most of the interior colour schemes were dark, and rooms were packed with furniture. A few styles overlapped during Victorian times: for example at the end of the era there was a Gothic revival, and buildings fashioned in Italianate and Queen Anne styles.

Edwardian (1901–1910)

The Edwardian period refers to the reign of King Edward VII and is influenced by eighteenth-century French décor, mostly famous for its neo-Baroque architectural style. Unlike the Victorian style, rooms were decorated in much lighter colour schemes, and

A typical Victorian style parlour.

A middle-class style
Edwardian bedroom.

decorative patterns were less complex. Art Nouveau and Art Deco were quite influential during the Edwardian era. Domed ceilings and wooden floors were very fashionable at the time.

Other Styles

Always remember that this is *your* dolls' house and you can decorate it in any style you like. Besides historical periods, dolls' houses may be built in a vintage 1940s, 1950s or 1960s style, and there are ultra-modern and contemporary styles for those who prefer a new, fresh and clean look. Some may go for a theme based in fantasy, or for something more festive such as Easter, Halloween or Christmas. Just leave it to the imagination!

SCALES

Dolls' houses and miniatures are also referred to as scale models. Scales define the ratio of the small model to the real, full-size object, and are expressed with a colon between the ratio, or as a fraction. The first number represents the model, while the second represents the units of the full-size object. Dolls'-house scales are represented by 1in as equal to 1ft.

Dolls' houses come in various scales: '1:12 scale', also known as '1in scale'; '1:24 scale', also known as '½in scale'; '1:48 scale', known as '¼in scale'; and '1:144 scale', also known as 'micro scale'. Micro scale is mostly used to decorate a

An ultra-modern combined living room.

Scales: a set of chairs in the same model but in different scales, starting from 1:12, 1:24 and 1:48.

tiny dolls' house for the 1in-scale dolls' house – in short, it's like having a tiny dolls' house for the real dolls' house.

In the past, dolls' houses rarely had uniform scales, but in the nineteenth century most dolls' houses were built in '1:16 scale' and '1:18 scale'. Nowadays the most common is '1:12 scale', where 1in on the dolls' house miniature equals 12in of the original object that has been copied. The smaller the second number of the ratio, the bigger the dolls' house model or miniature. Technically, in this case, a 1:12-scale model is twelve times smaller than the real full-size object.

Micro scale: a miniature dolls' house in 1:144 scale displayed in a 1:12-scale dolls' house.

TOOLS AND EQUIPMENT

To build a kit or a handmade dolls' house without any mishaps, it is essential that a suitable set of tools and supplies are ready to hand. The right tools make the process of building a dolls' house correctly much easier. Below is a list of the tools that will be needed to build a dolls' house, and their purpose. They can be found in hardware stores and craft shops, and can be purchased at a reasonable price.

Masking tape (1): Masking tape is essential when building a dolls' house. Ideally buy it in two sizes, wide and narrow. The wide tape is useful for keeping the dolls' house together when it is being dry built, and to cover the electrical wiring in the walls or floor grooves. The narrow tape covers windowpanes and small parts of the building that the builder doesn't want to paint while painting a surface area.

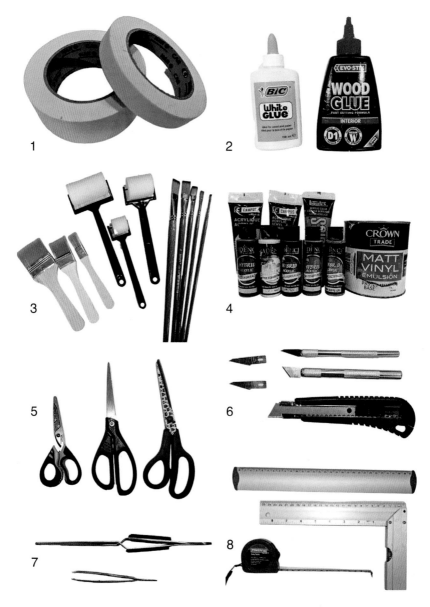

Glue (2): Two types of glue will be needed: wood glue for when the dolls' house is being constructed, and PVA glue or craft glue for floorings, ceilings and wallpaper. This glue can also be used for attaching soft furnishings such as curtains, and for covering furniture with fabric. Both types of glue give ample time to finish construction before it sets.

Paint brushes (3): Various paint brushes in different widths and sizes will be needed. One of the most used is a size 4 cotton roller brush, approximately 10cm (4in) in length; it is used to apply an even undercoat to the wall, ceiling and flooring panels. A small paint tray will also be needed to fit the roller brush.

Art flat paint brushes are quite important for this project – at least two to three between 40 and 50mm (1.6 and 2in) wide will be needed. They are used to paint larger surfaces such as roofs and shading façades. A paint brush for glue will also be needed. For smaller pieces, and accessories such as doors, windows, stairs and miniature furniture, a range of flat paint brushes from 5 to 20mm (0.2 to 0.8in) in width will be needed. The object that is being painted determines the width of the paintbrush – thus the smaller the objects, the smaller the width of the paint brushes.

CLEANING PAINT BRUSHES

It is important that paint brushes are cleaned well after use. Make sure that the brush used for glue is not used for painting.

Paints (4): Various paints can be used for the dolls' house project. The most basic is white emulsion paint, which is water based. It is used to give an undercoat to the project before papering, bricking and decorating any part of the dolls' house. Acrylic paints are also needed. They are water based and come in various colours, and are mostly used to shade and paint accessories such as windows, doors, roof tiles and even furniture pieces.

Scissors (5): Three types of scissors will be needed while working: general use scissors to cut cardboard, wallpaper and other craft material; fabric scissors for any type of fabric material and fibre; and small craft scissors to cut tiny craft pieces that bigger scissors can't reach. Make sure that all scissors are sharp and in good working condition.

WHICH SCISSORS TO USE

Never use fabric scissors to cut paper or other materials as scissors tend to lose their sharpness when used on tougher materials and textures.

Blades (6): Blades are useful for cutting thick cardboard or scoring into wood and metal. A retractable blade knife is ideal for big and tough objects, while a scalpel knife has a much finer blade that is more precise and easier to use; these are good for carving, or trimming edges. A hobby knife set, which has a combination of different blades, is also useful.

Tweezers (7): Tweezers can be used for holding on to very small objects, for example when picking up microscopic miniatures and putting them in place, especially when fixing them with glue.

Measuring tools (8): A metal 30cm (12in) ruler is essential, for measuring wallpaper, flooring boards, carpets and even ceiling paper; also when drawing precise straight lines on both paper and wood boards with a sharp pencil; when scoring wood or soft metal; and when cutting cardboard using a scalpel knife or retractable blade knife. A measuring tape is best for bigger objects such as the walls of the whole dolls' house. A hand-square tool is needed to get an exact 90-degree right-angle while constructing the dolls' house, and a 45-degree angle for roofs and for cutting mouldings.

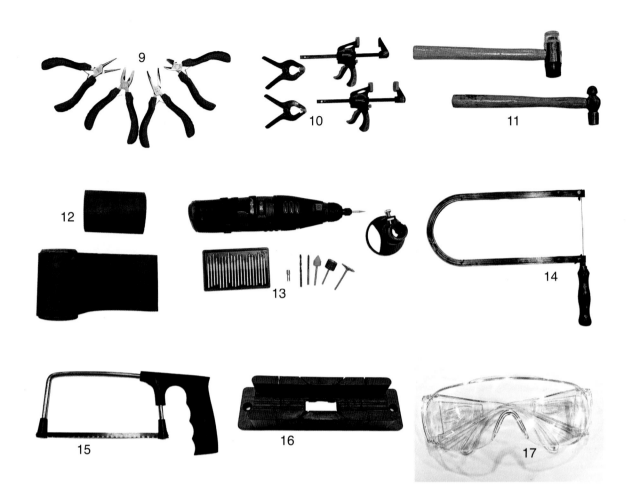

Pliers (9): Various pliers will be used for the dolls' house project. Small side-cutting pliers are useful to splice or cut wiring when installing the lights of the dolls' house. The long-nose pliers and the curved long-nose pliers are used for bending angles in wire or thin metal smoothly and also to pick up small screws. Combination pliers are useful for gripping, cutting and bending wire.

Clamps (10): Spring clamps and rapid bar clamps can also be used to keep walls, flooring and ceiling precisely in place. They are also ideal when gluing two pieces of wood tightly together.

Hammer (11): Some dolls' house kits will require a hammer, depending on the brand. A small, double-face soft rubber mallet will be needed for assembling the dolls' house and for setting dowels that require non-marring blows. If the kit has small nails or tacks then a small hammer is needed. Never use a soft rubber mallet to drive in nails or tacks as this will damage the tool.

Sandpaper (12): Sandpaper is especially useful for rough edges on wood boards. Sometimes kits need to be sanded down to have a smoother finish. The grit number indicates the abrasiveness of the material on the sandpaper. The higher the rating of the grit, the finer is the sandpaper. It is best to use a medium grit and a fine grit.

Power rotary tool (13): This multi-functional tool comes in both battery-powered and corded models, the different bits making it truly versatile. It is ideal for drilling tiny holes and scoring out grooves and channels in the floorboards when wiring the dolls' house. It is also suitable for cutting, carving, engraving, grinding, sanding, routing and even polishing.

Fretsaw (14): A fretsaw is a bowsaw that cuts intricate wood works such as tight curves, and in this project arches and circular openings. The range of blade sizes and teeth per inch varies depending on how intricate and detailed the wood needs to be cut.

Mini saw (15): A mini saw is a very useful for cutting wood quickly and accurately, such as in ceiling cornices, ceiling beams, frame mouldings, dado rails, floor skirting and low wall panelling. It can also cut other materials such as metal and plastic when the appropriate blade is used.

Mini mitre block (16): This block provides an accurate guide when hand cutting timber joints at 45- and 90-degree angles. Using a mini saw is a very efficient and easy way to cut the ceiling cornice and the floor skirting without any mistakes.

Safety glasses (17): Accidents do happen! When using most of the tools listed above it is important to remain vigilant and careful so no one gets hurt. It is also important to use safety glasses as these will help protect the eyes when cutting timber and drilling holes, just in case a piece of wood splits or the blade or drill bit breaks while working, sawing or cutting.

MATERIALS AND COMPONENTS

There are several materials and components that are essential in order to complete this dolls' house project, whatever its design, style and size. Most of these items are found from dolls' house suppliers, hobby shops and hardware stores.

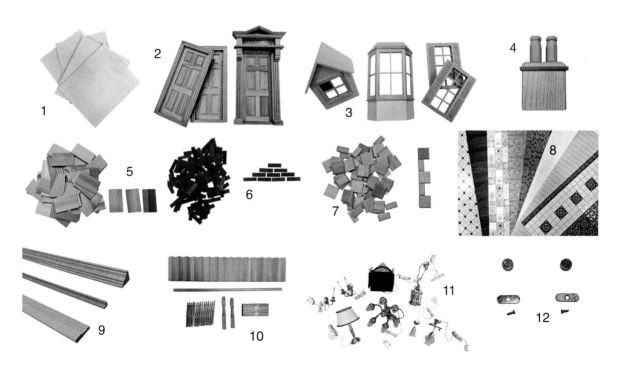

MDF (1): MDF is a type of fibreboard used to make the walls, ceiling and floorings. It comes in different thicknesses and sizes.

Doors (2): Exterior and interior doors will be needed for this project. The exterior door must match the period and style of the dolls' house. The number of interior doors needed will depend on the number of interior walls – for this project two to three interior doors will be sufficient. Door knobs and accessories are purchased separately.

Windows (3): The number of windows used for a project will depend on the style and size of the dolls' house. There is a wide range to choose from. Usually one window is sufficient for each room unless the room is quite wide, when two can be used. For this project a bay window will be used for the first room box, two medium-sized windows for the second room box, and two dormer windows for the third room box.

Chimney stack and pots (4): For this project one chimney stack will be needed and at least two chimney pots for the roof. More than one chimney stack can be used if the style and size of a dolls' house dictates.

Roof tiles (5): Roof tiles come in different shapes and materials. For this project individual triangular wooden roof tiles will be needed to cover the roof.

Brick slips (6): In this project, the walls of the first room box will have a brick effect. Card stock brick slips in red will be needed in two sizes to cover the outer walls.

Quoin bricks (7): Quoin bricks are needed for the second room box, which is on the first floor of the dolls' house. These are made out of wood and come in a mixed packet of two sizes or as a whole strip.

Decorative paper (8): Flooring paper, ceiling paper and wallpaper for four walls will be needed for each room. Decorative paper comes in various styles and sizes.

Mouldings (9): Various mouldings are available, most commonly the cornice, the skirting and the picture rail. These can be purchased unpainted and in various lengths.

Staircase (10): For this project, a staircase set will be needed, with hand railings, spindles and newel posts. Extra spindles, newel posts and hand railings will be needed to build a railing on the landing around the staircase well.

Lights (11): Various 12-volt lights are available. They come in different shapes and styles for ceilings, wall mounts and even as furniture and floor lampshades. The number of lights that are needed for this project is based on the number of rooms and the preference of the builder. For the ceiling-light fixtures ceiling roses can be added. A 12-volt transformer device and socket connector strip are also needed for the light fixtures to work.

Magnets (12): Small magnets are essential to keep the front of the dolls' house closed. They usually come in various sizes in a set of two attracting magnets or with a magnet, metal plate and screw.

CHAPTER 2

GETTING STARTED ON THE DOLLS' HOUSE

The start of the dolls' house is the most crucial step in its construction, whether it is a scratch build or a kit. Building your own dolls' house can be so much fun, and easy once you put your mind to it. One of my favourite methods is putting several room boxes together; it is one of the easiest ways to form a dolls' house, especially for a beginner. I will be using this method to illustrate how to build a three-storey Victorian 1:12-scale dolls' house.

PLANNING THE DESIGN

The best way to start building your very own design is to sketch the dolls' house on a sheet of paper. It doesn't have to be to scale or an exact match, but this will help you to visualise the dolls' house and have a clearer picture of what is wanted and needed. The benefit of building your own dolls' house lies in its originality, and that it can be designed in the style that suits you best.

The room boxes can be the same size or different sizes, depending on what is wanted. However, it is important that when they are put together, the depth and width of the dolls' house are the same. Usually a room box would be approximately 33cm (13in) wide, 33cm (13in) deep and 28cm (11in) high, but measurements can vary, depending on the builder's preference. A wide room box means that an interior wall can be added, so instead of having one large room, two smaller rooms can be made by dividing the room box with an interior wall with a doorway.

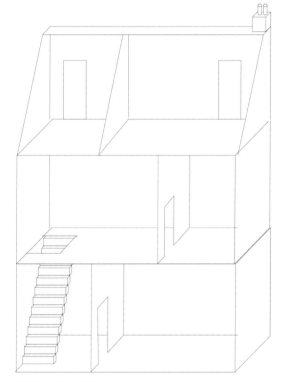

Building the dolls' house.

If building your own dolls' house I would suggest using fibre board, also known as MDF. Most dolls' house kits are made of MDF or plywood, which should be between 70 and 90mm (2.75 and 3.5in) thick. This type of wood can be found in a good DIY store. It is sold as a whole sheet but can be cut to the measurements needed. Be sure to measure each of the walls and floorboards accurately before cutting into the wood sheet.

An interior wall being added to a room box.

The dolls' house in this book is made from three room boxes with dividing interior walls. It is important that all three walls of a room box – the two side walls and the back wall – rest on the base, which is the floor. The side walls should cover the edges of the back wall, and the ceiling should cover the three walls at the top edges, or be placed inside the three walls flush at the top edges. The floor of the first room can be slightly wider as it will be the base of the whole dolls' house. As the second and third room box will be placed on top of the room box below, their fibreboard base can be 30mm (1.18in) thick; this will prevent the dividing ceiling and floor being very thick as compared to the walls.

Finally, the fourth wall is the façade of the dolls' house, and will include the front windows and main door. It should cover the four edges of the front of the room box(es), except for the room box that is set at the top.

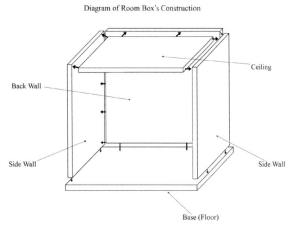

Constructing a room box.

The cut pieces of fibre board to be used to build the dolls' house.

The front opening against the room box.

Room box with a slanting roof and dormer window.

Every room box is built in the same way, and one placed on top of another, or next to another. The top-floor room box can be altered to accommodate a slanting roof: thus the front should be fitted between the side walls, and the top edges cut in a 45-degree angle. In this build the roof front will have two dormer windows.

The doors, windows, stairs and railings of the dolls' house are sourced separately in natural wood, and may be painted. They can be purchased from most dolls' house suppliers in their DIY section.

GETTING STARTED

Cutting an Opening for a Staircase

The ceiling of the ground-floor room box is also part of the floor of the first-floor room box, so if a staircase is to be added, be sure to cut an opening on both the panels that is big enough for the staircase to fit. These openings should be exactly the same, so that when the room boxes are put one on top of the other, the openings for the staircase match.

To cut the opening in the ceiling it is best to drill a small hole in each corner of where the opening should be, and then cut round these using a fretsaw. The tiny hole in each corner makes it easier to turn the saw blade from one side to the next, and to cut neatly. Make sure that the width of the floor opening is wide enough for the staircase to fit, and that there is enough headroom. This depends on the staircase that is being used. The length of the opening should be parallel with the second or third riser of the staircase from the bottom. On the first floor leave approximately a 5cm (2in) landing space. Before cutting the floor opening always allow for the walls' width.

Cutting the ceiling and floor of the room boxes for the staircase openings.

Cutting the Openings for the Windows and Doors

Having the windows and doors at hand is essential when cutting the openings in the interior walls and

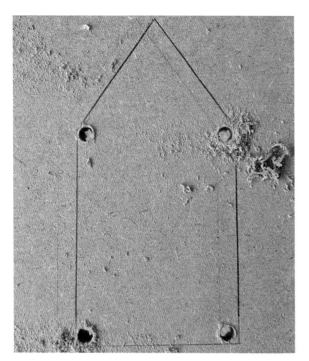

Drilling tiny holes in the wood panels before cutting the openings for windows and doors.

in the front of the dolls' house. With windows or dormer windows that are near to each other on the same wall, it is important that they are positioned at a right angle and that they are centred properly. Also make sure that the window openings are cut to face the room area, and are not cut in front of an interior wall's edge.

Drawing and taking measurements of the openings for the front door and bay window.

Measure the inside of the windows and trace the same measurements on to the façade. Drill four small holes in the corners of the traced windows, and using a fretsaw, cut round them to open the windows. Try the windows to make sure that the wall openings are big enough.

The Opening for the Front Door

If a step for the front door's threshold is to be added, and a small front pavement to cover the front, the opening for the front door must be cut at least 1cm (0.4in) above the lower edge, depending on the height of the rise of the threshold and the thickness of the wood that is being used for the front pavement. Just like the method used for the windows, measure the inside of the door and trace the measurements on to the wall for the doorway's opening. The bay window at the ground floor must also rest on the pavement. Be careful to measure and trace the opening accurately.

The interior door openings should be cut in the same way, only these can be cut straight down to the walls' lower edge. For the interior doors drill a hole at each top corner of the traced doors, and cut out the door openings with a fretsaw. Remember always to try the doors to see if they fit in their openings.

STARTING TO BUILD

Now that you know what is needed, it is time to study the kit and pieces. Hopefully this chapter will help you to build the dolls' house without any mishaps, whether you are building a kit or from scratch.

For those who are building a manufactured kit, a step-by-step manual for the dolls' house will be found with the kit. Go through the manual a few times before familiarising yourself with the actual parts and the construction of the building.

In every step-by-step manual the builder will find all the dolls' house parts that the kit should have. Make sure that all parts correspond to the manual, and that no parts are missing or damaged.

Illustrated sketch of the outside of the dolls' house.

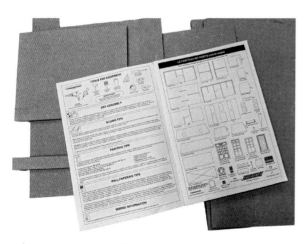

Dolls' house manual with the kit pieces.

the supplier or the manufacturer so they can replace either the whole kit or any parts that have been damaged or are missing.

For those who are building their own dolls' house, make sure to cut all the wall and floor pieces. It is important to know which wall and floor parts go where, and how they fit. When designing my own dolls' house I number the wood parts corresponding to the sketch that I have drawn.

DRY BUILDING THE DOLLS' HOUSE

Once the kit and pieces have been carefully studied, the dolls' house can be dry built. This is building the project without applying any glue to the pieces, and it is an important step as you can then see what the dolls' house will look like, and can check the pieces

Interior of a dry-built dolls' house.

Sometimes kits can be faulty, and as they are mostly made out of wood it is a good idea to check that nothing is damaged before starting to build. Wood can be split easily from the grain, and this can go unnoticed until you come to use it. If any parts of the kit are missing or damaged it is best to contact

The complete dry-built dolls' house.

more closely and how they fit before using glue. This will help you build more confidently.

Most manufactured dolls' house kits have grooves where walls need to slide into place. Sometimes these grooves need to be cleaned and widened slightly using fine sandpaper and a blade knife so the wall pieces can slide in easily to the bottom without splitting the groove. Check all window and door openings, and make sure that all the components fit in place.

Keep wide masking tape to hand, as it will definitely be needed to keep the walls in place while dry building. Masking tape is a very strong adhesive that can hold the pieces together, but will not leave any marks on the wood when it is peeled off when dismantling the dry-built dolls' house.

WHAT TO PAINT AND WHEN

Before we start building the dolls' house, an undercoat of paint must be applied to the walls, floors and ceiling. Even though most of the

Giving an undercoat to the room boxes with white emulsion paint using a roller brush.

undercoat paint is not visible to the eye and will be covered with decorative paper and wood panels, it is very important that this is done, for two specific reasons. First, wood is porous and has a grainy surface, especially plywood or natural timber, and after an undercoat of paint is applied, very often the grain of the wood lifts; this needs to be sanded down to achieve a smooth surface.

The second reason is that an even coat of paint applied to the dolls' house walls, ceilings and floors will give a lasting and smooth finish to the surface before the decorative paper is applied. This will also prevent any wood stains, which can damage the decorative paper at a later stage.

It is easier to paint the wall and floor panels of the dolls' house while they are still apart as this will give more access to cover everything. Both surfaces of the wood panels need to be painted, so it is best to start with the inside walls, floor and ceilings. Once the wood panels are placed on a clean surface, use the roller brush to give a light and even coat to the surface of the wood panels; then let them dry.

Painted dolls' house walls with grooves. The grooves should be clear of paint.

WHAT NOT TO PAINT

It is very important not to paint the edges of the walls and floors, or the grooves the walls need to slide into if a kit is being built.

Do not paint the inside of the door and window openings of the front panel of the dolls' house. If grooves, edges and component openings are painted, wipe them clean immediately with a damp cloth. Too much paint in unwanted areas will make it difficult to build the dolls' house, especially when a panel needs to fit into a groove or opening. There is no need to give a thick undercoat of paint on the dolls' house walls, ceiling and flooring on the first application.

After painting the two sides of the wood panels, let them dry off properly before giving them a second coat. If plywood or a natural type of timber

is being used, sand down the wood panels with a fine grit sandpaper to get a smoother surface. Clean the wood panels from any dust particles before giving the second coat of undercoat. It is important that the second coat is even and smooth, and covers the surfaces completely. Let the wood panels dry out for a couple of hours before building your dolls' house.

GLUING THE DOLLS' HOUSE

When all the walls, floors and ceilings have been given their undercoat paint, it is time to start gluing the dolls' house together. Make sure that the wood glue or PVA glue are to hand, and also a damp cloth to wipe clean any unwanted glue splashes.

Constructing the room box with glue.

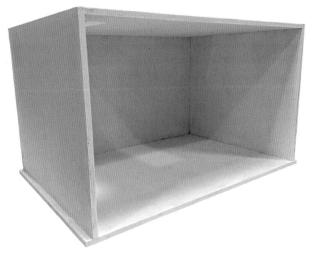

Room box painted with undercoat.

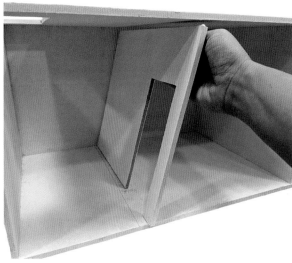

Fixing the interior wall to the room box with glue.

The three constructed room boxes placed on top of each other, forming a dolls' house.

Start with one of the side walls and the back wall, and glue these to the base, and where the sides of both walls meet.

While gluing the wall panels in place, use masking tape to keep the walls together.

Make sure that the walls stand at a right angle. If you are building a dolls' house kit that has grooves for the walls to slide into, the walls must fit properly into the bottom groove. If one of the walls is being stubborn to fit after applying undercoat to the wall, use a soft rubber mallet to tap it down into place. It is important not to use the rubber mallet directly on the edge of the wall – rather, place a piece of scrap timber on the edge that needs tapping down. This will prevent unnecessary damage to the edge surface. Glue the third wall to the base of the dolls' house and to the back wall.

As soon as the glue is set, glue the ceiling on top of the three walls: this makes the first room box.

Repeat this procedure with the other room boxes so they are built in the same manner. If interior walls are being added to the room boxes, these can also be pushed into place now and glued.

POSITIONING THE INTERIOR WALLS

It is best to mark the floor and ceiling where the interior walls are to be placed before gluing them. This will ensure that they are straight and at a right angle.

Number the room boxes when they are complete so they can be identified, so you know where they are meant to be in the project. Don't glue the room boxes together for now as it will be much easier to install lighting in the rooms.

CHAPTER 3

THE DOLLS' HOUSE EXTERIOR

Now that the dolls' house has been built, it is time to start working on the outside. The outside is seen first, so it must be eye-catching. It is easier to work on the outside of the dolls' house before focusing on the interior, especially if brickwork needs to be added to the front and side walls of the project.

By now you will have a clear picture in your mind of the style in which the dolls' house will be decorated. There are various ways to do this. It can be painted in one colour and given a plastering effect with some additional trimmings in a different shade. It can be given a brick effect, or it can have both plastering and brickwork combined. For this Victorian style dolls' house the latter method is used.

The dolls' house already has an undercoat of white emulsion paint, so now it must be decided which part should be bricked and painted. Most Victorian houses are all bricked, or the ground floor has bricked walls and the storeys above are plastered. Here, three room boxes make this dolls' house project, and the first room box, which will be the ground floor of the project, will have a bricked wall effect. The second room box, which will be placed on top of the first room box, will have a plaster effect; and the third room box – which is basically the attic – will be plastered and have roof tiles. It is easier to work first on the ground floor and move upwards, in the same way as a real house is built.

BRICKING THE EXTERIOR WALLS

Bricking walls doesn't necessarily mean that real tiny bricks will be used, but it will give the exterior walls an extra thin cover with the illusion that they are bricked. Most Victorian houses are built with red stock bricks. In this project, the first room box will have a red stone brick effect.

There are several ways to create this brick effect. Paper with a brick wall design can be purchased from most dolls' house suppliers, and comes in different brick patterns. There is also embossed brick cardboard, which has more detail than the normal flat patterned papers. These are quite easy to apply as they are pasted on in the same way as interior wallpaper. However, this method is really not suitable for use on exterior walls: because the paper is exposed to the elements, as time goes by, its

The first room box set at ground-floor level.

colours will fade. The paper can be sealed with an acrylic sealer to prevent this from happening, but it won't last forever, and sometimes the paper will even start to fall off and tear.

The easiest and most effective way to brick the walls is by using textured cardstock bricks. These bricks have a sanded texture, come in various colours, and are cut to scale. They are purchased in packs from dolls' house or railway model suppliers. It is simple to fix them into place with white PVA glue, and they can be easily cut with sharp scissors. They come in two sizes, the normal short size to cover flat surfaces, while the longer bricks are used for the corners.

Before starting the brickwork, paint the façade and the exterior side walls in the colour of the mortar, the paste that binds the bricks together. Mortars come in natural colours such as beige, grey and cream. For this project a grey colour was chosen as it will blend in much better with the red brick.

The ground floor façade will have a small bay window, so its roof should be glued in place and allowed to dry. Make sure that it is glued straight

Miniature red brick textured cardstock slips to cover the outside walls.

Covering the exterior walls with grey acrylic paint before adding the brick slips.

The exterior walls must be painted in grey to simulate the mortar colouring of the brick wall.

Applying PVA glue horizontally to the exterior wall with a paint brush before adding the brick slips.

Applying the first row of red brick slips to the exterior wall leaving a 1mm space between each brick.

Applying the second row of red brick slips over the first row in a pyramidal effect.

The complete bricked exterior side wall.

The front of the dolls' house against the bricked room box.

The two types of red brick slips. The short brick slips cover the walls, while the longer brick slips cover the wall and the corner.

Applying the corner bricks and the wall brick slips to the front of the room box.

Bricking the walls round the opening of the door and bay window, keeping to the same pattern.

Sealing the brick walls with PVA glue.

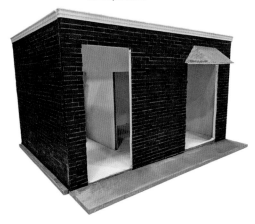

Fixing the top decorative moulding round the room box.

with enough room that the bay window will fit tight underneath it. Paint the bay window roof and the exterior walls that will have the brick wall effect – the two side walls and the façade – with grey acrylic paint using a roller brush or a medium-sized paintbrush. Make sure that the surfaces are totally covered with the grey paint, and then let the walls dry out for a couple of hours.

As soon as the walls are dry, start gluing the brick cardstock slips on to the painted surfaces, taking one wall at a time. Using a small paint brush, apply the white PVA glue to the painted walls horizontally in small sections. This will help to prevent the glue drying out until the whole section is bricked.

Start by building the exterior side walls, as they are the simplest and most straightforward to do. Just like building a real wall, start bricking the wall using the short bricks from the bottom left corner, going along the edge to the bottom right corner. The other rows will be stacked above the first row of bricks. It is important to leave approximately 1mm space between the bricks so the grey-painted mortar is visible.

Start bricking the second row of bricks after the first row of bricks is done. Remember to leave a space for the mortar between the first and second rows as well. The first brick of the second row should start at the halfway point of the first brick of the first row: ultimately this will give the wall a pyramidal effect. When the second row is finished, there will be a half brick space at both edges. Cut a brick slip in half and add the half bricks to the empty spaces at the edge.

Continue adding the brick slips to the glued wall in this manner, always leaving a 1mm space around the bricks. Brick the rest of the walls in the same manner and pattern until the top of the room box is reached.

The façade of the room box is bricked slightly differently from the exterior side walls because the front of the dolls' house is also its open side.

When putting the front of the dolls' house in place, it can be seen that the side of the front panel needs to be bricked as well to match the side walls. To cover the side and the front of the façade the long brick slips must be used, starting at the lower edge. Score the brick slip using a craft knife, bend it to a 90-degree angle so it is the same width as the side of the front panel, and glue it at the corner.

This should cover the whole corner of the front. The long brick slips are only used for the corners of the front. Continue gluing the façade with the short bricks in small sections as explained before, using the same method as for the exterior side walls. At the second row start with the short-sized brick slip at the corner; this will give the wall a pyramidal effect. Continue adding the brick slips to the row. Follow the same pattern by alternating the rows.

The façade of the room box will have a bay window and the main door, so the brick slips must be glued to the wall without obstructing the openings.

Make sure when gluing the slips to leave 1mm space for the mortar, and that the bricks are fixed in an even pyramid pattern. When the brick walls are completed, seal them with acrylic sealer, matt acrylic varnish, or even PVA glue diluted with a little water using a medium paintbrush.

A decorative wooden trimming can be added round the top of the room box. This will help to cover neatly the join between the ground floor and the first floor room boxes, and the transition from bricking to plastering. Measure the wooden trimming to fit the three exterior walls (the side walls and the façade). Paint the trimmings with acrylic paint in a colour that blends in with the rest. Add the wood glue to the top edge of the exterior wall, and fix the decorative wooden trimming to the walls leaving a 3mm allowance to cover the join with the first floor room box.

PLASTERING THE EXTERIOR WALLS

In this project, the façade and the exterior side walls of the second room box will have a plaster effect with quoin stone at the edges. This is one of the easiest ways to do the exterior of any dolls' house. If you want a more realistic looking dolls' house avoid bright colours for the exterior – rather, choose an off-white, cream, ivory, mushroom or bone colour emulsion paint. Colour paint can be purchased ready made, but you can mix your own colours by using white emulsion paint and adding small amounts of warm earth or a neutral colour of acrylic paint.

MIXING COLOURED PAINT

When mixing your own coloured paint, keep in mind the quantities of the paint used to achieve the colour just in case you need to mix more paint to match with the previous mixture.

The second room box, set at the first floor.

Acrylic paints, white emulsion paint and textured paint additive.

It is very simple to give the dolls' house a more realistic plaster effect. As soon as you are satisfied with the mixture of the coloured paint for the exterior, add small quantities of very fine sand. The amount depends on how rough you want the texture of the paint to be: the more sand added to the paint, the more textured it becomes. However, be careful not to add too much as the mix will get dry and the paint won't stick to the surface. I would suggest adding between 25 to 30g (0.9 to 1oz) of fine sand to 250ml (9fl oz) of paint. It is important that the sand is mixed well into the paint.

A textured paint additive can be used; this can be purchased from a hobby and model shop or from a dolls' house supplier. Brands may differ, so it is best to read the instructions to check the right amounts and measurements.

Adding the textured paint additive gradually while mixing the paint.

Once the textured paint is mixed and ready, paint the façade and the side walls of the room box exterior evenly using a roller brush.

To have a more realistic and detailed plastered surface, use a bristled paint brush and add more textured paint to small areas of the exterior walls.

Painting the walls with the paint mixture using a roller brush.

Applying more texture to certain areas of the wall for an uneven effect.

Let the paint dry for a couple of hours. Do not dispose of the unused remaining textured paint, but keep it in a sealed container so it can be used when needed.

Adding a Moulding Trimming and Quoin Block Slips

In the next step a moulding trimming will be added to the top edge, and quoin block slips to the side edges of the façade.

Most decorative mouldings and quoin block slips are made of wood and come in various lengths and sizes. These are available to purchase from dolls' house suppliers in the DIY section. First, cut the decorative moulding trimming to the same size as the front panel's width. Paint the moulding trimming to any preferred colour to add more detail. Fix the moulding trim to the top edge of the front with glue, and let it dry.

As soon as the decorative moulding trim is set and dry, the quoin block slips can be fixed to the side edges of the façade. Quoin blocks are decorative stones that are found at an angle of a building; they will give more detail and structure to the dolls' house. Quoin block slips come in two sizes. Starting from the left top corner, tight under the decorative trimming at the edge of the front panel, glue the square-shaped quoin block slip. The

Adding a decorative moulding and quoin block slips to the painted front for more detail.

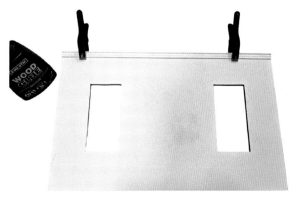

Gluing the decorative moulding to the top of the front wall.

second quoin block slip is half the square quoin block and should be glued right underneath the first slip at the edge.

Continue gluing the quoin block slips in the same pattern until the lower edge at the bottom is reached. If the last quoin block slip doesn't fit in the empty space, trim the block slip to size with a cutter and glue it in place. The last block slip should reach the top decorative trimming of the first room box at the ground floor level. Let the glue set for a couple

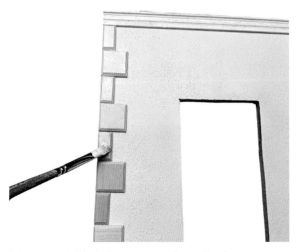

Gluing the quoin block slips to the sides of the front wall.

Paint the quoin block slips using a small paint brush.

of hours and then paint the decorative quoin block slips in the same colour as the building.

THE THIRD ROOM BOX: THE ATTIC

The third and last room box is the attic and will be placed at the very top. It will consist of a slanting roof with two dormer windows at the front and a chimney stack at the top.

Painting the Windows and Walls

The slanting roof is the front panel and the opening to the room box. Before fixing the dormer windows in place, give them an undercoat of white acrylic paint.

DORMER WINDOW FRAMES

Don't paint or fix the window frames of the dormer windows for now as work still needs to be done on the dormer window walls.

As soon as they are dry make sure that they are fixed straight with glue and in the right position, at the opening spaces of the window areas of the front panel. At this point keep the chimney stack to hand.

Start off by painting the exterior side walls and the exposed slanting wall edges using the plaster effect that was used for the second room box. Paint the walls with a small roller brush, and a narrow paint brush for the slanting wall edges.

The textured paint must also match the previous paint, so the room boxes will be the same colour when placed on top of each other. Using a small paint brush, and the same textured paint that was used for the exterior side walls, paint just the dormer window walls. Let the painted surface dry out for a few hours before starting with the roof tiling.

The third room box, set at the top.

The third room box: the dormer windows, roof tiles and chimney stack need to be added.

Painting the dormer windows with white acrylic paint.

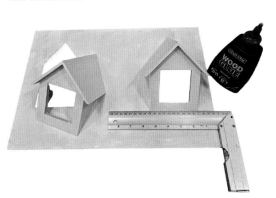

Fixing the dormer windows in place with wood glue.

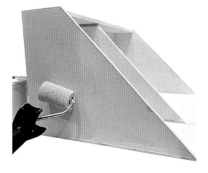

Painting the exterior walls with the textured paint with a roller brush.

Tiling the Roof

Miniature roof tiles come in different designs and materials. Roof tiles are available in full strips or individual tiles. The most common roof-tile shingles are the rectangular and the fish-scale designs. Some manufacturers make them in thick cardstock or in wood.

For this project, individual wooden rectangular roof-tile shingles will be used to make the roof; these can be purchased from most dolls' house suppliers in the DIY section.

In the next step, the roof-tile shingles will be fixed to the front panel of the roof. Start by applying small amounts of PVA glue with a small paint brush, horizontally from the lower left-hand side edge of the front panel to the other end.

Fix the individual roof tiles vertically next to each other on to the glued area in a straight line. Leave a 1mm gap between each roof tile when fixing them on to the edge of the front. If the last roof tile doesn't fit in the remaining empty space at the edge, cut it to the required width with a side cutter.

The second row of roof tiles is applied slightly differently. Using the same small paint brush, apply another horizontal line of glue above the first row of roof tiles and a quarter from the top of the roof tiles. Cut an individual shingle roof tile in half and place it at the edge, halfway above the first row of roof tiles.

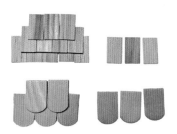

There are two types of roof tile: rectangular shaped roof tiles and fish-scale roof tiles.

Applying the first row of roof tiles with glue, leaving a 1mm space between each one.

Fixing the second row of roof tiles above the first row in a pyramid pattern.

Cut the roof tiles to fit round the dormer windows.

Completing the roof with the tiles laid up to the top edge.

Start with half a roof tile on the second row, to create the pyramid pattern effect. Keep adding the roof tiles in a straight line with a 1mm gap until the other edge of the panel is reached. The third row of roof tiles should start with a whole individual roof tile. At this point keep building the roof tiles in the same pattern and manner until the top of the front is reached.

TILING ROUND THE DORMER WINDOW

Fitting the roof tiles round the dormer window is an annoying task. However, keep to the pattern, and if necessary cut the roof tiles at an angle for them to fit. The first two rows should help as a guide to the roof pattern.

The top last row of tiles should be cut in half or to the required length depending on the empty space left.

Tiling the Dormer Window Roofs

Once the roof tiles are complete, the roofs of the dormer windows can be covered with the same type of roof tiles. Apply PVA glue on one side of one of the dormer window roofs, and place the first tile at

Applying the roof tiles to the roof of the dormer windows.

Both the dormer windows are tiled in the same manner.

the outer low edge of the roof. Keep adding the roof tiles in a straight line, just as the tiles were added on the roof itself. It will only take a couple of tiles to complete the first row.

The last tile of the row needs to be fixed to the inner edge, where the dormer window is joined to the roof panel, so it must be cut to an angle as required for it to fit. Don't worry if the tile rows of the roof panel don't match the tiles of the dormer window. Keep building the roof tiles of the dormer window in the same way and pattern as those that were applied to the roof. As soon as the first side of the dormer window roofs is complete, start with the other side. Try to put the same number of roof tiles on both sides of each dormer window so they look neat and even. Both dormer windows should have the same number of tile rows.

Painting the Roof

After leaving the roof tiles to set and dry, it is time to paint the roof. Roof tiles can be painted in a terracotta red or in a dark slate grey. For this project, dark slate-grey acrylic paint will be used. Using a medium-size paint brush, paint the roof tiles evenly with a thin coat of acrylic paint.

Two coats of paint might be needed to cover the roof completely. If there are unpainted areas in the gaps between individual roof tiles that the medium paintbrush couldn't reach, use a small old paint

Paint the roof with grey acrylic paint using a medium-sized paint brush.

An example of a chimney stack above a fireplace.

Placing the front of the roof on the room box.

brush to tap paint on to these areas. Leave the paint to dry for a while.

At this stage the roof is still not done as the dormer windows need refining, and the flat part of the roof will have the chimney stack and the battens with lead.

Installing the Chimney Stack

Before working on the battens, it is important to know beforehand where to place the chimney stack on the flat roof. Usually this would be at the centre edge on the left- or right-hand side of the roof, or at the centre edge at the back.

Always consider where the fireplaces are to be placed within the dolls' house. For example, if the fireplace is going to be against the left-hand side of the outer side wall, then the chimney stack must be placed on the left-hand side of the roof. Always try to keep the fireplaces under the chimney stack, as they would be in a real house. Make sure to have an idea of which room goes where within the dolls' house, and where the fireplace or stove would be placed within the rooms.

Ideally the chimney stack would be painted and completed at this point, before fixing it to the roof. The lower part of the chimney stack will be bricked in the same manner as the first room box. Paint the

Painting the chimney stack with grey and terracotta acrylic paints.

stack in the same grey acrylic paint that was used for the mortar, and fix the red brick slips starting from the lower edge, bricking it all round and moving upwards. Paint the top of the chimney stack and the chimney pots in terracotta or slate-grey colour. Once the chimney stack is ready, let it dry and set it aside.

Roof Battens and Lead

The flat roof will have roof battens with a lead effect. First, paint the flat part of the roof with acrylic paint in the same grey colour that was used for the roof tiles. For the battens I like to use bamboo skewers as they are the right thickness and are cheap to purchase. Real lead sheets can also be found for dolls' house projects. However, instead of using lead, I prefer to use aluminium foil cut into thin strips, especially if there are small children and pets in your household. Bamboo skewers and aluminium foil can be purchased from any grocery store.

The bamboo skewers are placed round the perimeter of the flat roof. Measure and cut them to the required size, and glue them on top of the flat roof all round the edge. Cut the aluminium foil into thin strips about 2cm (0.8in) wide.

With a small paint brush cover the strips with white PVA glue and place them over the bamboo sticks tightly and neatly. Even though the aluminium strip is wider than the batten, let the rest of the strip cover the roof and cut off any extra foil that would overlap the edges of the walls. Let it dry for a couple of hours. Using an old paint brush, dry brush with the same acrylic grey-coloured paint on the aluminium foil strips to take out the shine.

Place the chimney stack in place without gluing it. At this point, measure the spaces between each batten. The battens are fixed vertically and have to be spaced evenly. I usually use the width of the chimney stack to measure the spaces, depending on the width of the roof.

Mark the spaces where the battens have to be placed. Measure the length of the battens and cut the bamboo skewers accordingly. Make sure that the battens are glued into place straight and at a right

Completing the chimney stack with red brick slips.

Painting the roof of the room box with grey acrylic paint.

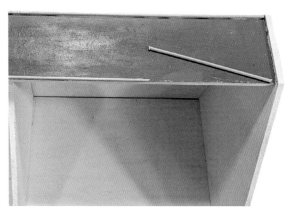

Fixing the bamboo skewers round the perimeter of the roof.

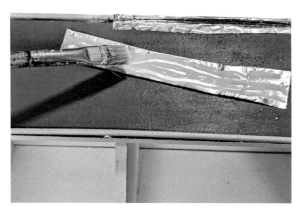

Applying aluminium foil strips over the bamboo skewers that are fixed round the perimeter.

Adding the vertical spaced battens to the roof of the room box.

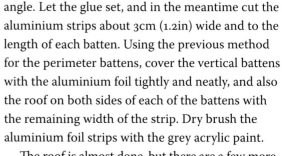

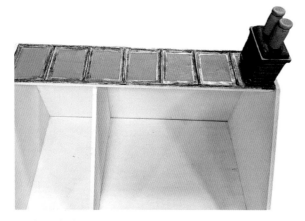

Finishing the battens with aluminium foil strips and acrylic paint.

angle. Let the glue set, and in the meantime cut the aluminium strips about 3cm (1.2in) wide and to the length of each batten. Using the previous method for the perimeter battens, cover the vertical battens with the aluminium foil tightly and neatly, and also the roof on both sides of each of the battens with the remaining width of the strip. Dry brush the aluminium foil strips with the grey acrylic paint.

The roof is almost done, but there are a few more details to add. As the battens are finished, the chimney stack can now be fixed in place with glue. Some edges still need to be covered with aluminium foil, to make the dolls' house look more realistic and authentic. Cut long strips of aluminium foil between 1.5cm and 2cm (0.6 and 0.8in) wide. The long strips will be cut in various lengths as you go along sealing the roof.

Applying the aluminium foil strip round the lower part of the chimney stack.

Fixing a long strip of aluminium foil above the top edge of the tiled roof.

Now that the roof battens and the chimney are fixed, the edges round the chimney stack and the roof can be sealed. Cut the strip with the length required to go round the chimney stack.

Glue the aluminium strip with half of its width on the lower edge of the chimney stack and the other half on the roof at a right angle; leave it to dry. The good thing about aluminium foil is that it is flexible and very easy to fold and shape into place.

Using the same method as before, seal the edges round the dormer window tightly and neatly with aluminium foil; this also includes the top ridge of the dormer window. Cut a bamboo skewer to size to fit a batten on the top ridge of the dormer window, and cover it with aluminium foil in the same manner.

Cut a long aluminium foil strip 1.5cm (0.6in) wide, and cover the edge of the top front panel – this will also cover the edge of the top half row of the roof tiles.

FOIL STRIP

The width of the foil strip can vary depending on the project. Always check the best width of foil to use for the dolls' house project to achieve the roof lead effect.

Adding aluminium foil over the top ridge of the dormer windows and round the joining edges.

As the glue sets on the new aluminium foil, once again dry brush it with grey acrylic paint to remove its shine so that it blends in better with the roof.

EXTERIOR DOOR AND WINDOWS

As the exterior of each of the room boxes comes closer to completion, it becomes clearer what the dolls' house will look like once they are put together. As most of the exterior work is done, the windows and exterior door can now be added. For this project a bay window and an exterior door with a window for the ground floor, and two windows for the first floor, are used.

Before painting the door and windows double check that they still fit in their openings, especially after the walls have been plastered and bricked. If the windows or door fit too tightly, just sand down round the inside edges of the walls' openings. Make sure that the accessories fit in their places properly.

By now the colour of the main door, the windows and the window frame of the dormer window will have been decided. It is important to study the accessories well, especially if they can be dismantled, so they can be painted without difficulty. Always

Door and windows accessories that are going to be used for the front.

Use masking tape to cover the windowpane before painting the wood.

Placing the door and windows in their openings to make sure that they fit well in place.

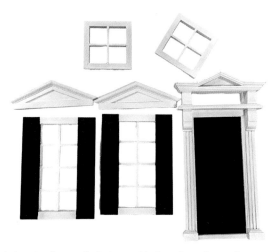

Painting the door and windows with the colour of your choice.

keep a narrow masking tape to hand, especially for those windowpanes that can't be detached from their frames and which need to be painted.

Most of the dolls' house DIY windows and doors have acrylic plastic instead of real glass. Unlike glass, acrylic plastic sheets can be easily scratched, so take care that this doesn't happen. If windows have plastic sheets that can't be detached from their wooden frames, cut thin strips of masking tape and cover the acrylic plastic on both sides before painting. This will protect the plastic sheet of the windows from being painted.

Using a small paint brush, paint the door and windows with two thin coats of acrylic paint in the colours of your choice. Keep a damp cloth to hand just in case unwanted or extra paint needs to be removed. Once the paint is dry, remove the masking tape from the windows. If there are parts that have been dismantled make sure that they are attached again in the correct order, and check if the windows and door still fit in the openings of the walls.

It is very important not to fix the windows or door in place with glue for the time being as wallpaper still needs to be added to the interior walls.

The Bay Window

In the Victorian and Edwardian eras bay windows were quite popular. A bay window is much bigger than normal windows, and it will give the dolls' house more character. Unlike normal windows the bay window protrudes from the existing wall, giving the room more floor space.

First paint the inside of the bay window, using a medium paint brush, in white except for the window frames and grilles; let it dry.

Turn the bay window so work on the exterior can be resumed. The bay window has three sections: a lower wall, three window frames connected to each other, and the roof, which is already glued to the façade.

The lower wall part of the bay window – which literally starts from the ground – must be bricked with the red stock brick slips, just as the exterior of the ground floor was bricked. First paint the lower part in grey to simulate the brick mortar, and then start bricking the lower part of the wall.

The thick part of the window frame that joins the three windows together can be painted in the same textured paint that was used for the walls on the first floor, so it will look as if it is made out of stone rather than wood. A small paint brush can be used to paint it. The inside frame and grilles of the windows can be painted in the colour of your choice, or in the same colour that was used to paint the windows. Also note that the inside of this section must be painted in the same way.

The roof part of the bay window must be tiled just like the roof. Just for the bay window, paint the under-roof trimming in grey acrylic paint. This part of the roof will be trickier as it is smaller and has two top ridges. Cut and fix the roof tiles just as the tiles of the roof were fixed. Once the glue is set, use a small paint brush to paint the roof tiles in grey acrylic paint.

The roof of the bay window is still not finished at this point. It is very important that the next step of this project is done after the façade has been bricked. For the two angled ridges found on the bay window's roof, two toothpicks should be used. Cut the toothpicks to the right measurement and fix them with glue.

Just as the method used for the roof, aluminium foil is used to cover the two ridges and where the roof tiles join with the wall. Cut thin strips of aluminium foil about 1cm (0.4in) wide. With a small old paint brush, add the PVA glue to the two roof ridges and their edges, and cover them neatly with the aluminium foil. As soon as it sets, cover the edges that join the roof with the exterior wall with the aluminium foil in the same way. Dry brush the aluminium foil with grey paint to take out the shine.

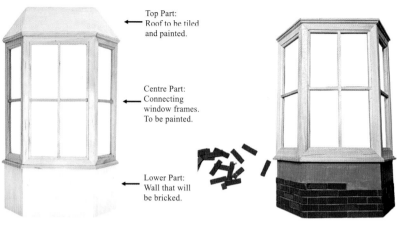

Top Part:
Roof to be tiled
and painted.

Centre Part:
Connecting
window frames.
To be painted.

Lower Part:
Wall that will
be bricked.

Painting the inside of the bay
window white.

Painting the lower part of the bay window
grey, and fixing the red brick slips with glue.

Painting the centre part of
the bay window with the
textured paint.

Tiling the roof of the bay window and
painting it with grey acrylic paint.

Adding toothpicks to the two roof ridges of
the bay window.

Covering the two roof ridges and the joint edges of the bay
window with aluminium foil strips.

Applying the paving on the outside door floor.

There is one last detail that needs to be added on the exterior after the bay window and main door have been fixed, and that is the outside flooring that supports the bay window and the main door's threshold. Most Victorian-era pavements were paved with blocks of uniform slabs. Thick cardstock can be used so the paving slabs can be cut individually and fixed on the flooring. Paint the front flooring in dark brown, and glue the cardstock slips in rows with a pyramid pattern, leaving a 1mm gap between each slab. Paint the cardstock slips in different shades of grey, and leave to dry.

Weathering the room boxes.

WEATHERING

The exterior of the dolls' house is basically complete once the outside door, windows and bay window are glued in place. All the walls have been plastered and bricked, the roof has been tiled, including the bay and dormer windows – but maybe the dolls' house looks too new and clean? A real house is always exposed to the weather and air pollution, and although some would prefer their dolls' house to look new and clean, others might think it more realistic if it looked more weathered.

To create a weathered effect several earth and natural-coloured acrylic paints will be needed – for example terracotta, moss green, burnt umber, yellow ochre, light grey, ivory or cream, and black. Sometimes these colours are mixed and blended with one another. A small sponge and an old medium paint brush are ideal for this purpose.

Starting from the roof, chimneys produce a lot of soot, so chimney pots and the stack must be blackened. To achieve the dirty look, dry brush with small amounts of black and grey acrylic paint. Don't apply too much. Take it slowly and gradually, and keep a damp cloth to hand to rectify any slight mistakes.

The roof tiles also need to be weathered. Just like a real roof, a mixture of different colour shades can be seen. Shading on the roof tiles can be conveyed by dry brushing with a medium old paint brush, and with water-diluted paints to give the roof more detail. For this, use a small paint brush, especially for the tiny edges and corners that are difficult to reach. When weathering with a paint brush the strokes should always go downwards. Never paint with an upstroke or from side to side.

Weathering the chimney stack by dry brushing with dark acrylic paints.

Diluting coloured acrylic paints with water before applying them to the plastered walls.

Dry brushing paint with a downstroke to achieve a more realistic roof.

Applying diluted green acrylic paint on the lower part of the brick wall.

Remember that gravity pulls downwards, rain falls downwards, so weathering must go downwards in the same manner.

Weathering should be applied to the plaster walls in the same manner, only the colour paints must be well diluted with water. Avoid dark colours. Use a sponge to create this effect, and a small paint brush for around the windows. Always keep in mind that the strokes must be downwards.

On the ground floor where the walls are bricked, weathering can be dry brushed on, and

detail and shading can be added with diluted paints. Shade the bricks individually if preferred. When creating a weathered effect, the closer you get to the ground, the darker the shades of colour need to be. The front paving needs to be weathered and dirtied as well. Use more greens and dark brown colours. Always blend the shading so there isn't a sharp contrast between the light and dark colours.

Remember to take it slowly – don't rush. If too much weathering is applied it can be corrected by using the colour that was first used when painting the dolls' house; similarly if too much weathering is added to the bricked walls, the unwanted extra paint can be easily removed using a damp cloth or a wet wipe as the brickwork was sealed before.

Weathering on a real building takes years to develop, so keep in mind that the dolls' house is being weathered in a much shorter time. Sometimes it can take a few days to weather a dolls' house before you are completely satisfied with it.

The complete dolls' house exterior.

CHAPTER 4

THE DOLLS' HOUSE INTERIOR

As most of the exterior of the dolls' house is complete, now it is time to focus on the interior rooms. Take a good look at the three room boxes: whether they are put together as a dolls' house or are still in single units, they are like a blank canvas. In this book the dolls' house consists of three room boxes with six rooms; most enthusiasts would have a sitting room and a dining room in the living area, a kitchen, the main bedroom, and maybe a bathroom.

By now you should have a clear picture of which rooms are to be placed in the dolls' house. Most dolls' house rooms follow the same pattern as in a regular house: the entrance rooms are usually the sitting and dining rooms, the kitchen is a smaller room, and the bedroom and bathroom are on the upper floors. Ideally keep a small notebook in which to write down favoured colour schemes, and a list of things and accessories and the number of lights to install in the dolls' house.

Decide which rooms to place in the dolls' house by marking them.

CHOOSING DECORATIVE PAPER

As soon as the rooms are designated to the dolls' house, the decorative wallpaper for the interior walls, floor and ceiling should be chosen. Everyone will have their own preference, but it is important to keep to the style and period of the dolls' house. For example, for a middle-class dolls' house don't choose an extravagant, fancy paper – be careful to keep it simple.

Victorian-style wallpapers have rich colours with big patterns. The sitting room is one of the most prominent rooms of the house, where residents would welcome guests, and can be decorated with a rich, fancy wallpaper. These come in a variety of

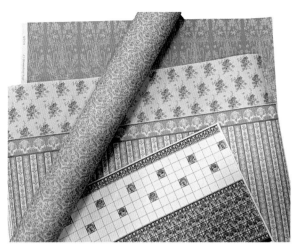

Choosing the right type of flooring, ceiling and wallpaper for the dolls' house.

It is essential to have the lights for the dolls' house to hand.

floral patterns, with different classical designs or stripes. Low wall panels in wood can be added to the papered walls. The floor can have floor tiles, or floorboards with carpets.

The kitchen can be quite plain, with partially tiled walls and a tiled floor. The other rooms can be decorated with patterned wallpaper in a smaller design. Bathrooms can also be decorated quite simply, with low wooden wall panels or wall tiles. Floors generally in the dolls' house can have a mixture of floorboards and floor tiles. Most decorative ceiling papers are textured or with an embossed pattern, and can fit any room around the dolls' house.

At this point the dolls' house lights can be purchased. Each room could have a ceiling light, wall lights and table lamps. If the dolls' house is to have one or two fireplaces and a kitchen stove, a fire basket with a working light might be added.

Once all the decorative papers and lights are collected together, work on the interior of the dolls' house can begin. It is important that all the lights, and especially the ceiling lights, fireplace lights and oven lights, are purchased beforehand as these must be installed while decorating the interior walls and floors so must be ready to hand.

APPLYING DECORATIVE PAPERS

The walls, floor and ceiling of each room are decorated in the same way, but it is important that the ground floor rooms are started first. Each wall must be wallpapered, including that of the opening front of the dolls' house. It is important to have enough decorative paper to cover the four walls, including an extra sheet in case of mishaps.

First measure the length and height of the three interior walls of the dolls' house. The side walls should be the same size. The back wall might be a different length, but the height should be the same.

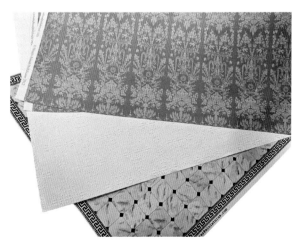

Preparing the decorative paper for the first room that is going to be decorated.

Measuring the walls, ceiling and floor of the room.

must be taken when cutting them. Make sure that the pattern is upright and straight. Each length of decorative paper sheet must show the same pattern sequence, so the three walls have the same pattern sequence from top to bottom. Try the sheets in the room for size just to make sure they fit before they are glued.

To fix the wallpaper sheets to the interior walls, a mixture of PVA glue and water is needed. Add

Also measure the floor and the ceiling, which should be the same. Even so, it is important that each section is measured individually just in case there are tiny discrepancies in the size.

Covering the Walls

Once the measurements of the first room are taken, cut the wallpaper of the three walls accordingly. Patterned decorative wallpapers give the dolls' house more warmth and colour, but great care

Using a medium paint brush, apply an even layer of the glue paste to the walls one at a time.

Cutting the decorative paper to fit the measurements of the room.

Fix the wallpaper to the wall. Make sure that the paper is straight and that no air bubbles are left between the wall and the decorative paper.

small quantities of water to the PVA glue, depending on its texture. The paste mixture shouldn't be too watery or too thick. Using a paint brush, add the PVA glue and water mixture evenly to one of the interior walls of the room. Make sure the whole wall is covered with the paste.

Place the wallpaper sheet against the wall very carefully, making sure it is straight. Make sure that the edges of the paper meet the edges of the wall. Very slowly smooth the wallpaper downwards against the wall. Make sure there are no air bubbles between the wall and the paper sheet.

DEALING WITH AIR BUBBLES

Air bubbles tend to appear when a sheet of wallpaper is being applied to a wall. The best plan is to keep a hair dryer to hand, and once the wallpaper sheet is pasted on and smoothed down, use the hair dryer to dry out the wallpaper against the wall: this will prevent air bubbles surfacing.

As soon as the first wall is covered with wallpaper, move to the next two walls of the same room and proceed in the same way. If one of the ground floor walls has an interior door opening leading to another room, apply the wallpaper sheet so that it covers the opening of the doorway. Once the sheet is pasted on the wall and the glue has dried, use a scalpel knife to gently cut out the section that covers the interior door opening.

Covering the Ceiling

Now that the interior walls of the room are covered with wallpaper, work can start on the ceiling. Embossed or textured ceiling papers complement the room. Most of these decorative papers come

Cut out the ceiling paper to fit the room's ceiling.

Using a scalpel knife, cut out the wallpaper from the doorway of the interior wall.

Apply the glue paste to the ceiling and fix the decorative paper in place.

in white or ivory and are easily cut. The best way to cover the ceiling is to put the room box upside down, or set the dolls' house on its side; this will give a clearer view and more space to work. Measure the ceiling and cut the decorative paper.

Make sure that the pattern of the ceiling paper is cut straight, and that a sheet fits properly before pasting it on. Just as with the wallpaper, paint the glue paste on to the ceiling with a paint brush, and fix the ceiling paper in place. Make sure that no air bubbles are trapped between the ceiling and the paper.

Covering the Floor

The last surface to cover is the floor of the room. There are several materials and designs to choose from: tiled floor papers, embossed cardboard sheets with a matt or glossy finish, wooden floorboards and textured floor carpeting. These can all be purchased from most dolls' house suppliers.

The same method will be used to apply the floor. Cut the floor sheet to fit the floor of the room, making sure that it is cut straight and that it fits in place. If a tile sheet is being used be sure that the tiles are divided evenly to fit the room.

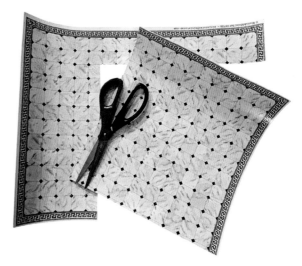

Measure the floor and cut the paper accordingly.

Wooden floorboards and textured carpeting are already prepared with a self-adhesive, so these don't need to be fixed with glue paste. They must be cut to fit, and the back paper peeled off gradually while smoothing the flooring into place, being careful not to leave any air bubbles between. Wooden floorboards can't be cut with scissors, but are easily cut with a fretsaw.

There are various floor coverings to choose from: floorboards, embossed and printed floor paper, and fitted carpets.

Fix the decorative flooring in the same manner as the ceiling and wallpaper.

Use the same method for the next room on the same floor.

The first room is complete, so work can start on the next room on the same floor of the dolls' house or room box. Follow the same method that was used for the previously decorated room to fix the paper for the walls, ceiling and flooring.

This dolls' house project is built using three individual room boxes, and each of their interiors is decorated in the same manner. This method only applies when decorating room boxes; when decorating a dolls' house kit, the ceiling lights of the ground floor rooms must be installed before the interior walls and floors of the first floor are decorated.

The front of each room box is part of the dolls' house façade, and the interior surface must also be decorated with wallpaper. If the room box has two rooms, then the interior of the front panel must have the same decorative wallpaper sheets as were used in the rooms.

The front interior must be a mirror image of the actual room box, so measure and fit the wallpaper sheets very carefully. With a pencil, draw a straight line where the interior wall divides the two rooms of the room box. Measure each of the two front sections of the interior walls to fit the wallpaper sheets. Cut the sheets upright and straight.

The three room boxes complete with ceiling, flooring and wallpaper.

The inside of the front panel must match the rooms of the room box.

WALLPAPERING THE INTERIOR OF THE FRONT OPENINGS

The interior of some parts of the façade of the dolls' house can be tricky, mostly on the ground floor and the roof because the dormer window and the roof of the bay window are protruding, so the front can't lie flat while the interior wallpaper is applied. This can lead to mistakes. Stack up two separate piles of books and put the front panel on top of these so the dormer window or the bay window's roof lie between them; this will make a solid flat surface.

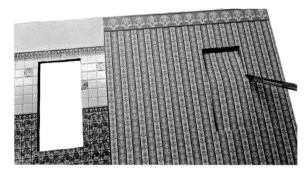

With a scalpel knife cut out the decorative paper from the front door and windows.

Using a paint brush, paste the PVA glue mixture to the interior wall of the front panel. Very carefully apply the wallpaper sheets one by one to the front panel neatly next to each other. Smooth away any air bubbles trapped between the wall panel and the wallpaper sheets. Once the wallpaper sheets are dry, cut out the wallpaper from the windows and door openings using a scalpel knife.

The same method can be applied to the other two front wall panels. Also the interior of the bay window on the ground floor and the dormer window of the attic can be decorated with wallpaper that matches the room.

DOORS AND WINDOWS

Once the walls, floor and ceiling are papered, a few more details may be added to the rooms to make them look more realistic before adding furnishings or accessories. In this project, the ground floor will consist of an entrance hallway and a sitting room. The first floor room box will have a dining room and a kitchen, and the second floor will consist of the bedroom and bathroom.

Now the main door, interior doors and windows should be painted. If they are not painted yet, make sure they are completed before fixing them in place. The door should have the door knobs or handles fixed in place before being installed. At this point have the staircase to hand, but do not fix it in place.

Measure and cut the decorative wallpaper for the interior of the front panel, and fix it in place with glue paste.

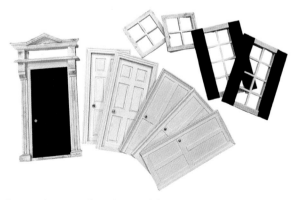

Prepare the painted windows and doors.

The First Room Box

It is always best to start from the ground floor and move upwards to the other floors. The first room box is set on the ground floor, and the first room is the entrance hallway, which will have a staircase leading to the first floor. It is a good idea to check that the staircase fits well in its place once the paper for the walls, ceiling and floor has been hung. Even though it is not decorated or fixed permanently in place, it is better to have it there so as to have a better idea of what the room will look like, especially if some fixtures need to be added around it.

The wall between the hallway and the sitting room has an opening for an interior door. Apply the wood glue round the outside frame of the door and fix it against the dividing wall. Depending on the

Fix the interior doors in the door openings with glue.

Place the staircase temporarily in place.

type of door that is being used, fix it so that it opens into the sitting room. Make sure that it is straight, and add the door trimmings to the other side of the wall to finish it.

Fix the bay window and entrance door in the openings of the ground-floor opening panel.

As the wallpaper is also complete on the inside of the front opening, the main door and bay window can be fixed in place. For the door, apply glue round the doorway, and fix it in the door opening. Make sure that it is fixed straight. Glue the remaining door-frame trimming on the other side of the door to complete it.

For the bay window, add glue round the window opening and the edges of the window's small roof. Fix the bay window to its roof and wall, making sure that its edges fit exactly under its roof, and that it is aligned with the opening in the wall.

The Second Room Box

The second room box is set on the first floor of the dolls' house, and will have a dining room and a small kitchen. Use the same method as was used for the first room box. If a staircase is to be added to this room box leading to the second floor, make sure to check that it fits neatly in place, but without gluing it in. The interior door should be painted and glued in place on the dividing wall. The door leading into the kitchen should open in the same direction as the one on the ground floor.

The façade of this room box has two window openings. Make sure that the painted windows fit in place. Apply wood glue round the outside frames of the windows, and glue both windows straight on the façade of the front opening. Then turn the front panel round and glue the interior window frames to the windows.

Fix the windows and the interior frames to the front of the first-floor opening panel.

The Third Room Box

The third and final room box is set on the second floor of the dolls' house. It is the attic room, and consists of the bedroom, though this might be divided to make a small bathroom in addition. In this case apply wood glue round the frame of the painted door and glue the door in place. The door should open into the bathroom.

The opening roof panel has dormer windows, which still need to have the window frames fixed in. Apply glue round the painted windows, and add them to the dormer windows. Once they are set, turn to the inside of the roof and glue the interior frames round the dormer windows.

The outside of the dolls' house is now complete.

Fix the windows and the interior frames to the dormer windows on the second floor.

FIXTURES, CORNICES AND SKIRTING

The last details that need to be added to the interior are the cornice and the skirting around each room. These hide the edges of the flooring, ceiling and wall papers, and make the room look neater. The cornice is placed where the ceiling and the walls meet, and the skirting where the walls and floor meet. These mouldings are usually made out of wood, which may be in its natural state, painted or even varnished.

Various wood mouldings: cornice, skirting and picture rails.

Fixing the surround of the stove in the kitchen before adding the skirting and cornice.

However, before adding these mouldings there are certain fixtures that must be put in place first. For example, if there is to be a fireplace or a fireplace breast in a particular room, these must be put in place before the cornice and skirting. Similarly a built stove surround in the kitchen must be put in place first. The fireplace pieces and oven must be to hand.

Miniature fireplaces come in different shapes and sizes, some complete with a surround and fire basket. The fireplace can be placed against the wall, or a fireplace breast installed behind it; this can be made with thick cardboard or wood. It is important to cover it with the same wallpaper that was used for the room. A fireplace breast must be installed before any cornice or skirting mouldings are added to the room because it reaches from the floor to the ceiling.

Miniature kitchen ovens or stoves may also have a surround, and this needs to be built and put in place before the cornice and skirting, which sometimes need to go round these fixtures.

Adding the Mouldings

When adding mouldings to a room, each side of the three interior walls must first be measured. Because the walls of each room are set at a right angle, the edges of where the mouldings meet at the corners should be cut at a 45-degree angle. Cutting mouldings is made easier with the help of the right tools, namely a miniature mitre box and a hand saw.

The angle on each moulding must be cut correctly. As soon as all the pieces of the cornice and skirting are cut, make sure they fit in place and

The mitre box helps to cut the wood mouldings at a 45-degree angle or straight.

Painting the cornice and skirting with acrylic paint.

that the angled edges at the corners meet neatly. Paint or stain the cut cornice and skirting pieces, then glue them in place with wood glue.

Start with the back wall ceiling cornice, then fix the interior side walls. Fix the floor skirting in the same way, starting with the back wall and continuing with the side walls.

When the room has a fireplace breast or similar, the cornice and skirting mouldings must go round the surround. It is important that the small pieces are measured and cut very carefully. Make sure that the mouldings are cut neatly, and that the angled edges meet before they are fixed with glue.

An example of a cornice and skirting round a fireplace surround.

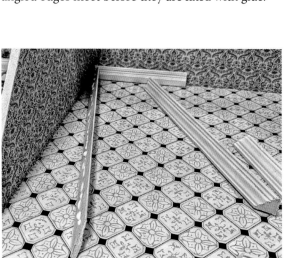

Fixing the cut cornice and skirting in the individual rooms of the dolls' house.

Sometimes fireplaces or stoves are placed in the interior side walls, and if lights are to be added to the fire baskets the wire would need to be hidden behind the floor skirting leading to the back wall; it is therefore important that the light and wiring are fixed in place before the skirting is glued down.

Use the same method to fix the cornice and skirting mouldings in all the rooms in the dolls' house. Different mouldings are available to decorate rooms – for example low wooden wall panelling, or a picture-rail moulding to add more detail to the walls. These are also cut using a mitre box and a hand saw, using the same method as for the cornice and skirting.

A set of magnets and metal plates to secure the front panels to the individual room boxes.

The picture rail divides the tiles from the painted area of the wall.

Screw the metal plates to the room box.

SECURING THE FRONT PANELS

The front openings of the house need to be secured to their matching room boxes, and the most efficient way of achieving this is by using magnets and metal plates, or two magnets.

These can be purchased from dolls' house suppliers from their DIY section. The metal plates must be fixed at the top edge of the room box. Depending on the size of the room box, two metal plates can be fixed to the top edge corners of a large room box or one in the centre of the top edge of a small room box. Each metal plate comes with a small screw.

Drill a shallow hole in the front panel the same width as the magnet. Fix the magnet in place with glue.

The magnets must be fixed to the front open panels of the room box, and must be in line facing the metal plates fixed to the room box. When fixing the magnets to the front inner panel it is essential to be cautious to prevent damaging the panel. Most magnets are a few millimetres thick, and the hole must be the same thickness as the magnet. Be very careful not to drill a hole that goes right through the front. The best way is to find a drilling bit the same width as the magnet, and to drill slowly until you find the right depth of the magnet being used. Glue the magnet in its place.

At this stage the interior walls, ceilings and floors of the three room boxes are complete, and the dolls' house looks more real.

The doll's house is complete with decorative paper, cornice and skirting.

CHAPTER 5

LIGHTING THE DOLLS' HOUSE

Adding lights to the dolls' house gives warmth and realism, from the lit ceiling chandelier to the glowing fire basket of a fireplace. Lighting a dolls' house can be intimidating and challenging to a few, but once there is an understanding of how it works, and by following these simple instructions, it will be quite easy to do.

There are two types of light fixture that can be installed in a dolls' house: battery-operated lights and 12-volt electrical lights. Battery-operated lights are easy to fix but they are bulky, most of them give a white light, and the battery runs out quite quickly. 12-volt electrical lights are more practical and can be installed in two ways: using either copper tape or an electrical socket connector strip. As dolls' house light bulbs are tiny and have a very low voltage, it is essential to use a transformer device. Supplies for both these methods can be purchased from the lighting section of any dolls' house suppliers. For

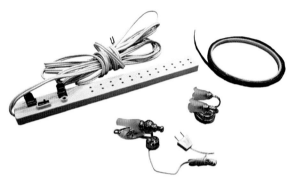

Dolls' house lights have two types of fixture: battery-operated lights have a tiny switch on the fixture itself, while electrical light fixtures must be connected to an electrical socket strip or to copper tape.

this project, 12-volt electrical lights with the socket connector strip method will be used as it is easier to install, especially for a beginner.

Planning is most important when adding lights to the dolls' house. Depending on the size of the room, each room could have a ceiling light, a pair of wall-mounted lights, and free-standing lights – so it is important to have a clear picture of the number and type of lights each room should have.

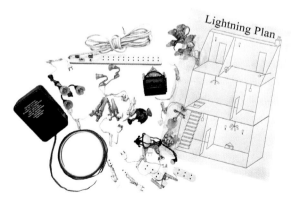

Preparing the lighting accessories prior to installing them in the dolls' house.

HOW MANY LIGHTS TO USE?

Adding lights to a dolls' house gives a warm atmosphere and makes it more realistic, but adding too many lights to a room may overpower the special details that you would like to bring out. Always consider the size of a room and its purpose, and avoid having too many lights in a small room, or just one or two lights in a much bigger room.

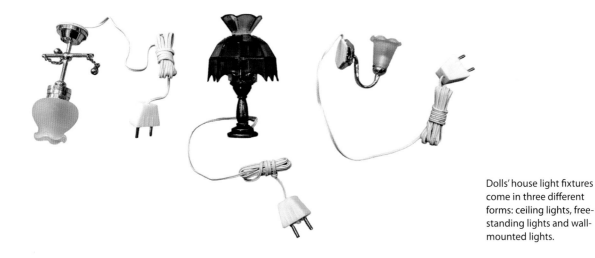

Dolls' house light fixtures come in three different forms: ceiling lights, free-standing lights and wall-mounted lights.

Marking each light fixture on a simple dolls' house sketched diagram will indicate the number of lights needed, the design of the decorative light fixtures, and where to place them.

CHOOSING THE LIGHTS

There are various beautiful chandeliers and wall scones with decorative frosted shades that would fit perfectly for the Victorian era, and a wide range of free-standing lights such as table lamps and floor lamps. Always bear in mind in which period or era the dolls' house is to be set, and never go for modern accessories in an older styled dolls' house. In the early Victorian period homes were still lit with candles in candlesticks and chandeliers. Later on, oil lamps and gas lights were used.

Ceiling-light fixtures are available with different numbers of bulbs. Those most commonly used for a dolls' house contain between one and six bulbs, while wall-light fixtures usually have one or two bulbs. Most light fixtures have screw-in bulbs or push-fit bulbs that can be replaced when needed. Avoid those light fixtures where the bulbs can't be replaced.

It is generally best to choose lights for a room according to its size and purpose. In a sitting room

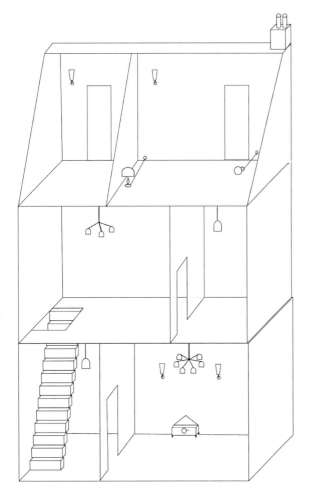

A lighting plan sketch will help decide what lights will be added to the dolls' house.

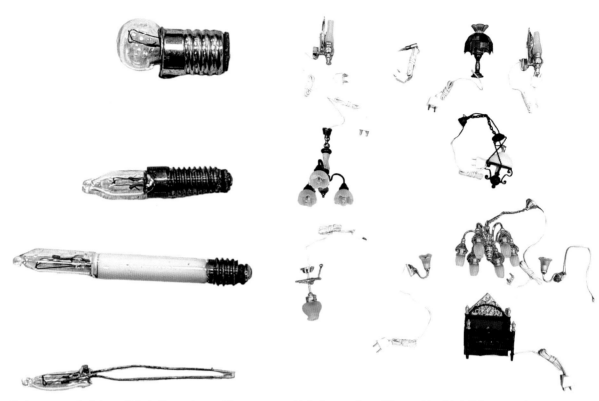

Various types of miniature light bulbs can be used for the light fixtures: pea-shaped bulbs, screw-thread bulbs, candle bulbs and flame-tipped bulbs with wire ends.

Light fixtures that will be used for this dolls' house project.

or dining room consider a chandelier with six bulbs and a pair of wall-mounted light fixtures to go against the back wall. A two-bulb ceiling light would be best for a smaller room such as a kitchen. Bedrooms could have a four-bulb ceiling-light fixture and a pair of free-standing lights. In the narrow space of a hallway or staircase well, wall-mounted lights are ideal. If the dolls' house has one or two fireplaces and a kitchen oven, adding a fire basket with a working light would give a realistic effect.

It is best to assemble all the lights before decorating the dolls' house with decorative paper. When building a kit or renovating a dolls' house, decorative paper and the lighting system are done simultaneously, but because this dolls' house is built with room boxes they can be done separately.

TRANSFORMER DEVICE AND SOCKET CONNECTOR STRIP

Having the decorative light fittings is important, but for the lights to work in a dolls' house a socket connector strip and a transformer device must be used. Each individual light fitting is wired, and at the end of the wire there is a small two-pin plug. The socket connector strip is the terminal to which each of the lights is attached. Most of these terminal strips contain twelve sockets, a fuse and an on-off switch.

If the dolls' house contains more than twelve light fittings, or the wire of the light fixture is too short to reach the terminal connector strip, then extension connector strips must be added. These usually have one or three sockets that can be attached to the terminal socket strip and to the light fixture, and are very useful and efficient to use. Never try to stretch a light fixture's wire to reach a socket – the wire within the light fixture is fragile and can tear very easily.

The transformer device is fundamental when it comes to lighting a dolls' house. Normal household voltage is between 220 and 230 volts and is too high for 1:12-scale dolls' houses, which use 12-volt lights. A transformer device takes a given input of voltage, which in this case would be around 230v AC (alternative current), and changes it to an output of 12v DC (direct current); it therefore decreases the electrical voltage for the dolls' house.

There are various 12-volt transformers that can take different amounts of wattage, which means they can only take a certain number of light bulbs. Dolls' house transformer devices are measured according to the number of bulbs and not the number of light fixtures. This means that although the dolls' house may have only twelve light fittings, in all it might contain 30 bulbs. The most common transformer devices take sixteen, 32 or 50 bulbs, which can be purchased from any dolls' house supplier.

The terminal strip has a fixed cable that has two metal fork prong connectors at the end, which need to be attached with screws to the transformer device. The transformer is then plugged into a household electrical socket to light the dolls' house.

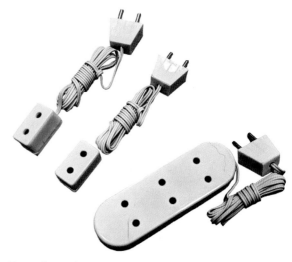

Types of extension connector strip.

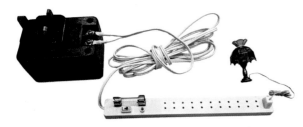

The lighting fixture must be plugged into the electrical terminal strip and the wiring of the socket strip connected to the transformer. The transformer must then be plugged into the household electrical socket.

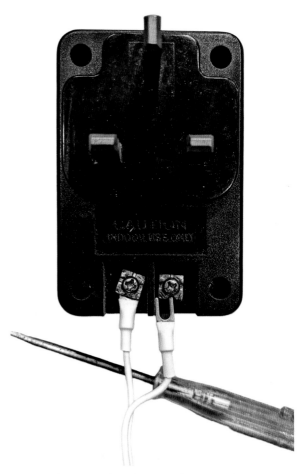

The metal fork prongs from the terminal strip must be connected to the transformer.

The label on the transformer will indicate how many bulbs it can take and the type of voltage that it can receive and give.

INSTALLING THE LIGHTING SYSTEM

As soon as the light fittings, the transformer device and the socket strip connector are assembled, the process of installing the lights can begin. Always start from the ground-floor rooms and move upwards to the storeys above. When building or renovating a dolls' house, installing the light fittings and adding decorative paper must be done simultaneously because the wiring of the ceiling-light fixture on the ground-floor level goes through the ceiling of the room, crosses the flooring on the first-floor level and goes out through the back wall. As the ceiling of the ground floor is the same wood panel as the flooring of the first floor of the dolls' house, the ceiling-light fixture of the ground floor must be installed before adding the flooring to the room on the first floor. The same method is used for all the ceiling-light fixtures in the other rooms and for the other storeys above.

Installation of Ceiling Lights.

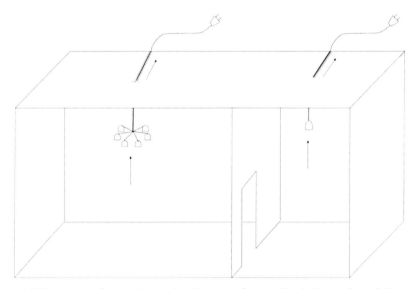

A dolls' house room diagram showing how the wiring from a ceiling light goes through the ceiling, crosses the flooring of the room on top, and goes out through the back wall. If it is a room box it just crosses the top surface.

This dolls' house project consists of three room boxes put together, so the method is basically the same but the flooring on the first and second floors won't be affected.

The first step is to mark with a pencil where the light fittings need to be fixed, and where holes and channels need to be opened up for the wiring to go through. Starting with the ceiling-light fixture of the first room on the ground-floor level, establish where the centre of the room is, because most commonly a chandelier would hang from this point. The best way to find the centre of the room is by measuring the ceiling's edges from outside the room box. Technically it would be like measuring the flooring on the first floor. If the room box is divided into two rooms it is important to mark where the dividing interior wall is. Always take into account the thickness of the room's walls.

Once the length and width of the room's ceiling have been measured, divide each measurement by two to find the centre of each of the ceiling's edges. There should be two equal pairs of measurements. Mark with a pencil the centre of the ceiling's side at the edge. Using a ruler, draw a straight line from one side to the opposite side of the ceiling, forming a cross. The centre of the room is where the two lines cross, and this is where the ceiling light should hang from. Always double check the measurements to make sure that the marked centre is correct before drilling the tiny hole at the centre.

Using the power rotary tool with a 3mm drill bit, drill a straight hole in the ceiling. Then a channel needs to be made for the wire to lie in so the surface remains flat, especially if it is the flooring of the first floor of the dolls' house. Draw a straight line from the hole towards the back of the room box. Open a channel across the drawn line with the power rotary tool using a rotary bit. The channel must be about 3mm wide and 2mm deep. It is important that the groove is not too deep, as the wood board will lose its structural integrity and can break very easily.

If a dolls' house is being built or renovated another tiny hole needs to be drilled in the back wall on the first floor where the channel groove ends

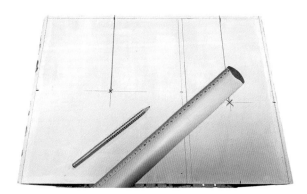

Measuring the top of the room box to find the centre of the rooms.

Drilling the hole for the ceiling lights and opening a channel for the wire.

Measuring and drilling the holes for the wall sconces.

Drilling a tiny hole in the lower part of the wall behind the fireplace for the fire-basket light.

The same type of holes should be drilled for the fire-basket lights in the fireplace, or the stove surroundings of the dolls' house. The holes should be prepared in the wall as low as possible behind the fire basket itself. If the fireplace or stove is set in the side wall of the room the wire needs to be hidden behind the skirting of the wall and a tiny hole drilled in the corner of the back wall very close to the floor. Take note that the wiring of any additional light fixtures added to the dolls' house must go through the back wall. It is essential that lights are set correctly in their place, and that any wires are hidden.

CEILING ROSES AND DECORATIONS

Ceiling roses give a nice touch and add extra detail to the ceiling. They come in various styles and sizes. The choice of ceiling rose depends on the size and style of the room, and even the size of the ceiling-light fixture. Ideally the ceiling rose would be slightly bigger than the circumference of the ceiling-light fixture. They can be purchased from any dolls' house and miniature supplier.

to enable the ceiling-light wire to exit. The same method is used for all the ceiling-light fittings in the other rooms. In a few dolls' house kits the tiny holes and channel grooves for the lighting system have already been done.

Wall-mounted light fixtures are much easier to fit in dolls' houses. Ideally, wall lights should be added to the back wall as this gives the room a more attractive glow. If a pair of wall sconces are added to the wall, make sure that they are set at the same height and are symmetrical. Mark the wall with a pencil where the wiring of the wall-light fixtures should go through, and very carefully drill a tiny hole with the power rotary tool using a 3mm drilling bit.

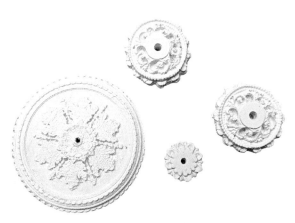
Various ceiling roses that will be used for this project.

Fixing the ceiling rose to the centre of the room's ceiling. It is important that the holes in the centre of both are in line.

Decorative corner mouldings added to the room's ceiling.

Most ceiling roses are made out of plaster or resin and come with a tiny hole at the centre for the electrical wire to pass through. If not, a small hole must be drilled at the centre of the ceiling rose with the power rotary tool. Ceiling roses can be painted in the same colour scheme as the room, or to match the cornice and skirting.

Once painted, the ceiling rose must be fixed to the ceiling of the room before the ceiling-light fixture is added. Turn the room box upside-down so as to have a better view of the ceiling. Apply PVA glue to the ceiling rose, and fix it at the centre of the ceiling. The tiny hole in the ceiling and the hole in the ceiling rose must be in line with each other so the wiring of the ceiling-light fixture can pass through to the floor above.

Decorative ornaments can also be added to the corners of the ceiling. These complement the ceiling rose and give more detail to the ceiling, especially if the decorative paper is not embossed. They can be fixed on the ceiling with glue between the cornice and the ceiling rose. Let the glue dry thoroughly before setting the room box upright again.

INSTALLING THE WIRING FOR THE LIGHT FIXTURES

Before installing the light fixtures check that they are in good working order. Make sure that the bulbs are screwed into their holders properly. Test every light fitting separately and ensure that they work as they should, without flickering or any one light being dimmer than another. Connect the light fixture temporarily to the socket connector strip and transformer device in order to test the lights.

Every light fixture has a long wire that needs to be fully extended before installation, and the tiny two-pin plug at the end of the wire removed. Using a pair of grip pliers, remove the pins from the plug and gently tug the two wires free. Twist the two loose wires together so it will be easier for the wire to pass through the tiny holes. Keep all the plugs and metal pins safe for later use.

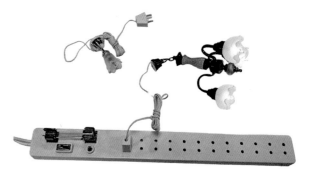

Testing the light bulbs of each light fixture separately.

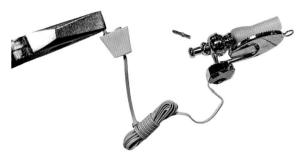

To install the light fixtures, the plug at the end of the wire must be removed by pulling out the pins with a pair of grip pliers.

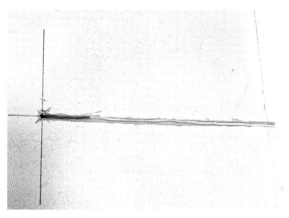

Place the wire in the open channel at the top of the room box or in the flooring of the room above.

Ceiling Lights

Starting with the first ceiling light, insert the wire of the light fixture into the ceiling rose's hole and pull very gently from the other side until the light fixture has reached the ceiling. All light fixtures are supplied with an adhesive pad to attach them. Peel off the paper from this pad and secure the light permanently in place to the ceiling rose. As soon as the light fixture is fixed in place, move to the other side and ensure that the wire is placed straight – without any twists or bends – into the opening of the groove. In a dolls' house the wire must go through the hole in the back wall, but in this case the wire must go to the back of the room box. To keep the wire secured in place, cover the wiring

Cover the wire in the channel with masking tape.

Pass the wire of the ceiling light into the fixed ceiling rose.

channel with masking tape. The same method should be used for all the ceiling lights in the other rooms of the room boxes.

Wall-Mounted Light Fixtures

The method for installing all the wall-mounted light fixtures is very simple. Insert the extended wire into the back wall and gently pull the wire from the other side until the light fixture reaches the back wall. Peel off the paper from the adhesive pad attached to the light fixture, and fix the light to the wall. Ensure that the fixture is straight and upright.

Fix the wall lights into the back wall.

The Lighting for the Fireplaces and the Stove

The method for installing the lighting for the fireplaces and the stove will depend on which wall they are to be positioned. If the fireplace is placed against the back wall, the extended wire of the fire basket will be taken through the tiny hole in its back and out through the back wall. Tug the wire gently from the back of the room box or dolls' house until the fire basket is positioned nicely within the fireplace.

If the fireplace or stove is set against one of the side walls of the room, the fire basket must be set in

Pass the wire of the fire basket into the fireplace and into the back wall.

its place within its alcove. The wire of the fire-basket light fixture must be hidden behind and against the flooring within the surrounding. Then the wire must be taken towards the lower corner of the back wall and into the tiny hole. From the back of the dolls' house or room box, gently pull the excess wire remaining without moving the fire basket from its place. Hide the wire behind the wooden skirting of the room.

Free-Standing Light Fixtures

The free-standing light fixtures can also be added if their exact position in the room is known. Furniture pieces can be used to measure the length of the wiring needed in order for it to remain inside the room. All wiring for the light fixtures must go through the back wall.

Place the lampshade on a piece of furniture in the right position, and pass the wire through the back wall.

Connecting Up the Light Fixtures' Wiring

At this point, all the light fixtures are installed in the right place. The room boxes should be built on top of each other for the final time to form a dolls' house. Once they are in place, turn to the back of the dolls' house to connect the wiring to the socket connector strip and to the transformer

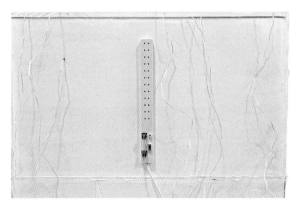

Fix the terminal socket connector strip in the centre of the back of the dolls' house.

Anchor the ends of the wire in the plug with the pins.

device. All the wirings of the light fixtures must be connected to the socket connector strip, so ideally the strip should be fixed in the bottom part of the dolls' house towards the middle, and preferably at the back of the second room box. The connector strip has an adhesive pad at the back: peel the paper off and mount the strip vertically in its place.

The light fixtures' wires are quite long, so to keep them neat and tidy, cut the extra wiring to the appropriate length to fit the socket connector strip terminal. Don't cut the wires to the exact length, but leave at least a few centimetres allowance for the plugs. All the plugs and pins need to be added to the wires of the light fixtures. Slip the wire into the

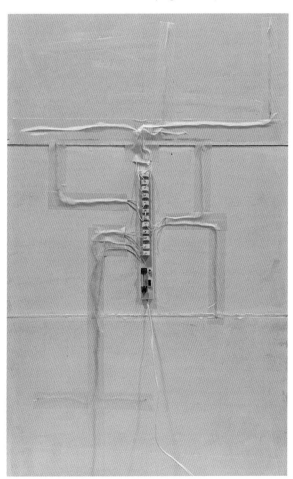

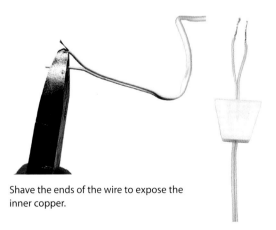

Shave the ends of the wire to expose the inner copper.

Pass the ends of the wire into the small plug.

Insert the plugs into the socket connector strip and cover the wires neatly with masking tape.

plug, and with the side-cutter pliers open the wire so both ends are loose again. Very gently shave both the loose wire ends by approximately 5mm (0.2in) so the copper strands within are exposed. The copper strands of the wiring have to have contact with the two pins for the electric current to pass. Using the gripping pliers, anchor the two ends of the wiring with the metal pins in the plug. Make sure that no copper strands are exposed outside the plug.

The dolls' house is now fully lit.

After adding all the plugs to the light fixtures' wiring, connect the plugs to the socket connector strip terminal. Tidy the wiring at the back of the dolls' house by covering them neatly with masking tape.

Connect the wiring of the strip terminal to the transformer device with a screwdriver to tighten the pads of the transformer to the fork prong connectors of the terminal strip wire. As the transformer device passes an alternative current, the wires can be fitted both ways as long as they remain separate. Connect the transformer to the closest house electrical socket. If the connector-strip terminal has an on/off switch, turn it on and the dolls' house will finally be lit.

PRECAUTIONS AND SAFETY MEASURES

Always remember that precautions and safety measures are essential when installing electric lights in a dolls' house. Most brands recommend that none of the dolls' house electrical components are suitable for children under fourteen years of age. It is important that adults are present at all times if children are handling electrical components or are in the vicinity during the installation of the dolls' house lighting system.

Make sure that the working space and area are dry from any moisture or water. Switch off and unplug any electrical components when they are not in use. Check bulbs and electrical connections if a light fixture is not working.

Never leave a dolls' house lit without any surveillance or if unattended by an adult. Remember that these lighting accessories can be dangerous if not used properly, as negligence and misuse can result in serious damage, fire, electrical shock and injury.

CHAPTER 6

STAIRCASES

Most dolls' houses contain one or more staircases: they give the dolls' house a touch of realism and detail. Different types of staircase can be used for a dolls' house. The most common is straight, though a few have an 'L'-shaped staircase, or a 'U'-shaped staircase with a central

An example of a 'U'-shaped staircase in a dolls' house.

landing. Usually a staircase is found in the hallway at the centre of the dolls' house, but this depends on the design of the dolls' house itself. There is also the spiral staircase that can be used for both older and more modern periods. The curved staircase and the bifurcated staircase are used for grand entrances found in larger dolls' houses.

In this project a straight staircase will be used as it is the simplest, with only one flight of stairs leading from one floor to another. The staircase is set on the left-hand side wall of the first room box at ground-floor level in front of the main door entrance and leads to the first floor.

STAIRCASE PREPARATION

Most staircases come in kit form, with spindles, newel posts and hand railing, and sometimes even with separate treads. Staircase kits and parts come in bare wood and can be purchased from dolls' house suppliers from their DIY section. Because the measurements of the rooms will vary, sometimes the staircase needs to be adapted and shortened by one or two steps to fit in its place properly. Make sure that the staircase is set at a 45-degree angle, and that the rise of the first step at the bottom is set at a right-angle with the flooring. The tread of the last step at the top should be flush with the landing on the first floor.

First the staircase needs to be painted and assembled before being fixed permanently in its

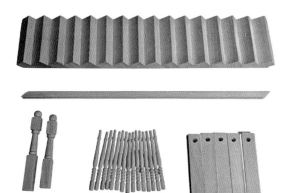

An unassembled staircase kit for a dolls' house with railings, treads, spindles and posts.

Adding the decorative embossed paper to the staircase soffit.

place. There are various ways of decorating and painting a staircase. Staircases in the Victorian period were made of thick wood such as oak, so the staircase and its components can be stained in a dark wooden stain or paint. Alternatively the staircase can be painted in white acrylic paint, and the spindles, newel posts, hand railing and treads stained in a dark natural wooden shade. Another option is to have the staircase, treads, newel posts and hand railing stained in a dark stain and the spindles painted in white or ivory. In this project the staircase and spindles will be painted in white, and the rest of the components stained with a dark oak

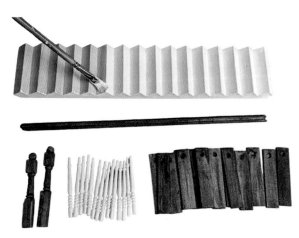

Painting the staircase in white acrylic paint and staining its components.

stain. This will add distinctive detail between one step and the other.

Paint or stain the staircase and all the components, and leave to dry. The stair soffit also needs to be painted, especially if it is visible. 'U'-shaped and 'L'-shaped staircases are an example of this. Decorative paper can be used for the stair soffit, preferably matching the ceiling paper of the room. Measure the stair soffit, and cut the decorative paper accordingly. Apply PVA glue to the stair soffit using a small paint brush, and paste the decorative ceiling paper smoothly to it; allow to dry.

ASSEMBLING THE STAIRCASE

Adding the Treads

Once all the staircase parts have been painted and stained the staircase can be assembled. First the treads must be placed on each step, and this must be done very carefully. Usually the treads come with a tiny hole on one of the sides where the spindle will be fitted.

The staircase can be set against either the left- or the right-hand side of the interior side walls in the room. In this project it will be set on the left-hand side of the room. This means that the treads must be placed with the nosing set on the right-hand side of the staircase and at the front of every step. Make sure that the hole on the tread for the spindles is set on the right. On the left-hand side, where the staircase rests against the wall, the tread and the run of the step must be parallel on top of each other. The tread nosing must not protrude beyond the side of the staircase against the wall. Fix the treads on the

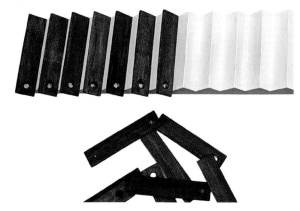

Fixing the treads on the staircase with PVA glue.

Adding the Railing

Once the spindles are glued in, the hand railing can be put in place. This is usually set at a 30- to 45-degree angle. If the staircase has been altered or shortened the railing also needs to be cut. Measure the length of railing that is needed to cover the space between the newel posts, and cut it at the necessary angle. Most staircase kits come with a handrail cut at a 45-degree angle at both ends, so a mitre block and small handsaw will be needed to cut these precisely.

To make sure that the railing is fixed right on top of the spindles, place the staircase temporarily in the dolls' house and set the newel posts in their position with some tacky glue underneath to keep them in place. Angle the railing between the newel posts, and glue it on top of the spindles. Make sure that all the spindles at the top are fixed properly inside the hand railing from underneath. Leave the railing glue to dry and set.

The staircase is now assembled.

run of the staircase with wood glue and leave to dry for a few hours.

Installing the Spindles and the Newel Posts

Next to be installed are the spindles and the newel posts. The spindles must be fixed in their tiny holes on the treads of the staircase, and the two newel posts placed at ends of the staircase. First glue in the spindles, making sure they are straight, and leave to dry. The two newel posts are added once the staircase is in its permanent position: the post at the bottom must be fixed on the flooring at ground-floor level, and the other one on the top landing on the first floor. It is a good idea to keep them to hand, especially when it comes to measuring the railing.

Fixing the hand railing on top of the spindles.

DECORATING THE STAIRCASE

The construction of the staircase is now complete, however, a very important detail can be added to it. In the Victorian era staircases were carpeted, with solid brass rods to keep the carpet in place. This gave a rich look and an extra warmth to the house. In this project the staircase will have a decorative runner complete with stair rods and holders. Staircase runners come in various colours and patterns, and stair rods and holders are available that will fit most staircase kits.

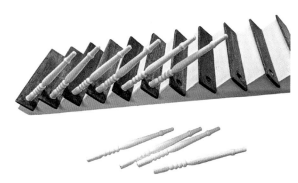

Fixing the spindles straight on the staircase with glue.

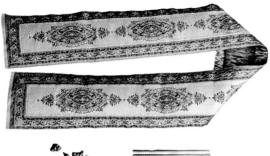

Rods and holders to keep the runners in place on the staircase.

Mark with a pencil where the holes of the rod-holder pins are to be drilled in the stairs.

Just as on a real staircase, stair rods are fixed at the lower edge of the staircase risers. Stair-rod holders keep the rods in place so they must be secured at both edges of the step. First measure and mark with a pencil both step edges, where the rod holders are to be placed. The holders must have enough space for the rod and the runner to fit between them, and they must be exactly the same. If the rods are too long, these can be cut to the required measurement with a side cutter. Drill tiny shallow holes with a 2mm drill bit into the staircase risers for the holders to fit into.

HAVE THE RIGHT DRILL BIT

Depending on which miniature staircase rods are being used, make sure that the drill bit being used is not too wide for the holder's pin to fit, because then the holder will be too loose for the tiny hole and will fall out. It is a good idea to take a scrap of timber block and try out different drill bits until you find the right measurement for the staircase holder so that it is a tight fit and won't fall out.

Glue the holders into the tiny holes of just one side of the staircase. It doesn't matter which side goes first. Wait until the glue has dried completely,

then position the stair rods. It is important to add the stair rods before gluing both the holders, because otherwise it will be very difficult to put the rods in place.

Once the holders are fixed tight on the first side of the staircase, put one end of a rod into a fixed holder. Then take another loose holder, place it on the other end of the rod, and fix the holder in place with a small amount of glue. Fix the rest of the rods in the same manner and leave to dry.

Very gently pass the staircase runner behind the rods, and shape it according to the staircase. Once the staircase carpet is in place, the staircase and the newel posts can be glued permanently in place.

Add the rod holders to one side of the whole staircase.

Measure and cut the rods accordingly and add the rod holders to the other side of the staircase.

Place the runner between the rods and staircase and position neatly.

Stair-Rail Guard

At the end of the staircase, like any real house, a stair-rail guard must be built round the staircase opening with posts, spindles and hand railing. Measure the perimeter of the opening where the stair-rail guard must be, and cut the hand railing accordingly. Paint and stain the parts of the stair-rail guard to match with the staircase. Place the newel posts at the corner edges of the perimeter and glue them, and space the spindles equally between the posts. Place the hand rail above the spindles and between the newel posts to complete the stair-rail guard.

At this point the staircase is complete. The same method is applied for any staircase in the same project or in any other dolls' house.

The complete stair-rail guard set on the first floor of the dolls' house.

FALSE DOORS

Sometimes a staircase can take up quite a lot of space in a room or hallway, especially in a small dolls' house. Some would prefer not to have a staircase fitted at all in their dolls' house to save the extra space – but a dolls' house might appear less realistic if there is no means of getting to the other floors.

Another option instead of a staircase is to have false doors. These are simply miniature doors that lead to no particular room, but give the illusion of maybe leading to a staircase. They create a certain curiosity, and give the dolls' house more depth and perspective. Unlike the interior doors used in the side walls, the false doors don't open – they are shaped as a door on one side and are flat on the other side. They are mostly found in bare wood and can be purchased from a few dolls' house suppliers.

In this project false doors will be used on the first and second floor instead of building a staircase. It is important that the feature looks realistic. A false door is usually placed in the back wall of the room, though it doesn't matter where in the wall – it could be at the side or in the centre.

Paint the false doors and add door knobs to match the other interior doors.

False doors look very realistic on the back wall of a dolls' house room.

The complete staircase fixed in the entrance hall.

Paint the false doors in the same colour as the interior doors that do work, and add the same type of door knobs. This will make them look less conspicuous and no different from the real doors.

Once the false doors are painted, place them against the wall. Planning for false doors has to be done beforehand, as the doors must be fixed in place before the skirting is added around the room.

CHAPTER 7

FURNISHING THE DOLLS' HOUSE

The construction of the dolls' house is complete, so now the rooms can be decorated with furniture and accessories. Dolls' house furniture is available for every room, and in any style and period. Readymade furniture pieces are the most popular and come in various price ranges, styles and colours; they may also come in bare wood, which is quite an advantage. Even though the furniture is already built, it still needs to be painted or stained. Some dolls' house brands and artists also offer dolls' house furniture in kit form, where the furniture pieces need to be assembled with glue, then painted and decorated. Furniture pieces are available from dolls' house and miniature suppliers, and from individual artisans.

Decorating a dolls' house with furniture needs to be planned. Two main factors that must be considered are how big the room is, and correspondingly how much furniture will be needed. Beginners tend to purchase furniture pieces without knowing exactly where to place them, or without knowing even if they would actually fit at all, probably because they imagine the room to be bigger than it actually is, or they don't realise how big the miniature furniture really is, or they try to fit in every furniture piece that they like, and not because it is needed for their particular project.

Some examples of a finished furniture piece, another piece in bare wood, and the last piece in kit form.

CHOOSING FURNITURE PIECES

A few aspects need to be considered before choosing furniture pieces for the dolls' house. Furniture style is one of the most important, as pieces must match with the period and atmosphere of the dolls' house; it is therefore essential to stay faithful to the design of the project. This dolls' house will be decorated in the late Victorian period style, and will represent a middle-class environment. Victorian dolls' house furniture pieces are quite popular and easy to find.

As mentioned above, another factor to be aware of is how many furniture pieces can actually fit in a dolls' house room. Sometimes when furniture pieces are put in place it becomes clear that they are too big, or there are too many for the one room. Take note of the room's floor measurements and of the furniture pieces, and add a few single pieces gradually, rather than putting in all the furniture at once. This will give a better idea of how the room will look, without cluttering it up with unnecessary pieces.

In the Victorian era furniture was mainly made out of mahogany, oak and walnut, and sometimes in light wood. When decorating a particular room in a dolls' house try to use the same finish for all the furniture pieces, or the same shade of colour. There is no need to choose just the one type of colour, stain or finish for the whole dolls' house, but it will definitely look better if the furniture pieces in the same room match.

Always start with the obvious and most important furniture pieces for any one particular room. This will help to give a good picture of how they fit in the space available without overcrowding the room. It doesn't matter which room you start with, but it is a good idea to focus on one room at a time.

A few examples of Victorian period dolls' house furniture.

A dolls' house decorated in the Victorian period style.

Furniture for the Hallway

The entrance and staircase landings can be somewhat restricted in space. Mostly the walls are decorated with accessories, though a few furniture pieces can still be added to give that extra detail.

In this project the entrance hallway with a leading staircase has its limitations. The furniture pieces chosen for this area must be petite and dainty, while still giving that welcoming atmosphere. In the Victorian period, hallway stand pieces were quite

Dolls' house furniture pieces finished in mahogany, oak, walnut and light wood.

Furniture pieces that are ideal for an entrance and a hallway.

popular to hold parasols, walking sticks and hats near the entrance. A side table with a framed wall mirror on top fits very well.

For any part of a hallway, no matter on which floor of the dolls' house, small furniture pieces are good fillers. A small pedestal table underneath the staircase with accessories on top can give that extra touch. A grandfather clock is perfect for a narrow space and looks quite glamorous. Flower arrangements on a plant stand are ideal on a staircase landing.

The Parlour or Drawing Room

The sitting room is one of the most prominent rooms in the dolls' house. In the Victorian era the sitting room was known as the 'parlour' or 'drawing room', and it was the heart of the house. It was used to welcome guests and entertain the family in the evening, and it would be furnished with valued furniture pieces.

In this project a fireplace has been set in this room already. A settee and two matching armchairs are placed looking towards it, with a coffee table between them. If a combined sitting/dining room is preferred, a pedestal round table with two more dining chairs can be added instead of the coffee table. An attractive cabinet and a bookcase would look very effective against the walls. Gentlemen would sometimes conduct their business in the parlour, so a desk would be appropriate. If the room is spacious a piano might be included: these instruments were quite popular, especially for evening entertainment.

The Breakfast Room

In smaller residential houses there would be a breakfast or luncheon room rather than a dining room. This room was used during the day for breakfast and lunch, and even dinner in the evening for the family. It was found in close proximity to the service room, and was not used for entertaining guests. In this project the breakfast room is on the first floor when going up the stairs. It is furnished with a small table with four matching chairs. A sideboard or china cabinet could be added as part of the dining area. Small furniture pieces can be used to add more detail.

Parlour furniture in walnut that includes armchairs, a settee and a cabinet.

The breakfast room has a small mahogany dining table with four chairs and a side table.

The Kitchen

In the Victorian era the only purpose of the kitchen was for cooking. It would have been the smallest room in a middle-class residential house, and as it was never visited by guests or outsiders, it didn't have any fancy detail. Only the necessary equipment for food preparation would be found, the kitchen stove being the most important, in this period often made out of cast iron. In this project it is set in a built alcove in the back wall of the room. Other features might include a small washing sink in a cupboard or a butler's sink; hanging wall shelves, which were very common in a Victorian kitchen; and a side table or cupboard that would be used as a working surface and to store food.

The Master Bedroom

In the Victorian era the main bedroom, or the master bedroom, was considered to be one of the most important rooms in the house, decorated with beautiful furniture pieces. Generally the bed would have been made out of solid wood with elaborate carving; sometimes it was of cast iron or brass. A wardrobe, dressing table and chest of drawers would have been included, though in a smaller room not all furniture pieces would have fitted – in this case a chest of drawers with a mirror on top would have been used as a dressing table. A small fireplace was essential to keep the room warm during cold nights. Small furniture pieces can be used to occupy any empty spaces, such as a bedside table, an armchair, maybe a small pedestal table.

The most important pieces in a kitchen are the stove, a butler's sink, a side table or cupboard, and hanging shelves.

For the small bedroom a single bed, a combined wardrobe and dresser, and a desk will be used.

A traditional Victorian ceramic white bathroom set with a claw-foot bath, a wash basin and a chain-pull toilet.

The Bathroom

Porcelain white bathrooms were quite common in the late 1880s. By that time plumbing was found in most households. A small room would have been used for the bathroom, situated at a short distance from the sleeping quarters. Some porcelain bathrooms were also decorated with a colourful design.

Boat baths, also known as 'bateau baths', were free-standing bath tubs that were very popular in the Victorian era. The bathroom washing basin came in various designs: fixed to the wall and supported with two metal brackets, most commonly with a vanity unity built around it; and later versions had a matching porcelain pedestal underneath for support.

The water closet, which is now known as the toilet or lavatory, was made to resemble the chamber pot. The high-level toilet would fit perfectly for the period; the cistern was mounted high on the wall supported by two brackets, and its water pipe leading to the toilet was exposed. A long chain was used to flush it. The toilet would have matched with the rest of the bathroom. Wall-mounted shelves and a cupboard could also feature in the bathroom.

More Room Options

A nursery, study room or library and separate dining room could be added if the dolls' house is larger and has more rooms.

A room with furniture pieces that can be used for a library or study.

REVAMPING FURNITURE PIECES

There is always the possibility that you can't find the right furniture piece for a project dolls' house. Maybe the piece is exactly what you wanted but the colour or stain of the wood doesn't match with the rest, or the fabric doesn't blend well with the décor or the colour scheme in the room. Sometimes repainting it, or adding a little detail to a cheap furniture piece can turn it into something unique.

Bare-wood furniture is easy to stain or paint as the natural wood can be customised as required: it can be painted with acrylic paint, or stained with any type of wood stain. After painting or staining it is important to finish the piece with a coat of varnish. There are various acrylic varnishes available, the most common being matt, satin and gloss.

A readymade furniture piece that has been sprayed or painted can be challenging to repaint. Most of the time paints don't stick well to furniture

Staining bare-wood furniture with a medium-sized paint brush and dark stain.

Sand down the polished furniture before repainting it with a new coat of paint.

surfaces, and the smallest scratch will make the piece look very untidy. The best way to repaint it is to start by sanding it down. First remove any door handles or drawer knobs, and if possible any doors. Sometimes doors are very difficult to remove so they have to remain in place. If the furniture piece has plastic sheet instead of glass make sure to remove it gently before sanding down or painting. Plastic can be damaged and scratched very easily.

Use a medium-grit sandpaper to sand down most of the polished spray from the surface of the furniture, and then use a fine-grit sandpaper to smooth it down.

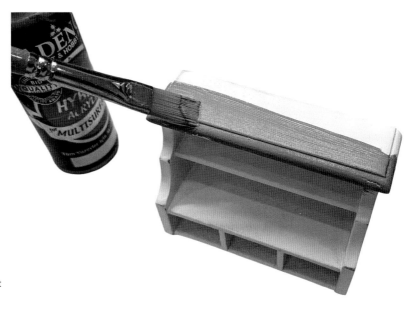

Paint the furniture piece with acrylic paint and a medium-sized paint brush.

The complete furniture piece after it was repainted.

Clean any dust particles from the surface, and with a medium-sized paint brush, paint it with a light coat of paint in the desired colour; let it dry.

Give the furniture piece a second light coat of paint. Thick coats of paint will obscure the detail of the furniture, and can prevent doors and drawers from closing neatly. Let the paint dry thoroughly. Give a coat of acrylic varnish to the furniture piece to seal the paint, and let it dry for a couple of hours. If the furniture piece has any plastic sheet and knobs, glue them back in place.

Adding detail and decoration to a piece of furniture can enhance it and make it more unique. Small jewellery embellishments and waterslide decals make great additions to furniture pieces. They can easily be painted over to blend better with the colour of the furniture.

SOFT FURNISHINGS

Soft furnishing is another phrase for textiles, and describes any type of fabric that is used around the house, from the rich fabric covering the settee in the parlour to the small tea towel in the kitchen. Soft furnishings are one of the most important factors in any household as they keep the home warm and comfortable. In the Victorian era they were also used to display the wealth and status of the family.

Soft furnishings will be found in every room of a dolls' house, and they can be easily handcrafted to suit individual taste.

Reupholstering Furniture

Sometimes the right furniture for the room is not upholstered in the shade or pattern of fabric that

Miniature soft furnishings for the dolls' house.

blends well with the room's colour scheme, and the best way of tackling such a problem is to change the fabric completely. It is important that the fabric chosen to reupholster a settee or an armchair is not thick: silk, polyester and cotton are ideal. If the upholstered fabric needs to be fancy make sure that the pattern is tiny. Patchwork fabric from a haberdashery or craft shop is ideal to reupholster miniature furniture.

To reupholster a miniature settee or armchair, first study the furniture, in particular how the fabric is fixed to the wood. Generally the upholstery is glued to the furniture and is made out of fabric for the outside, cushioning foam for the inside and cardboard for the back of the cushioning. Very gently remove the fabric and padding from the chair frame without tearing it. Separate the fabric from the foam and the cardboard.

The armchairs, settee and chairs that will be reupholstered.

Fabric with a small design and pattern is ideal for upholstering miniatures.

Remove the upholstery from the furniture slowly.

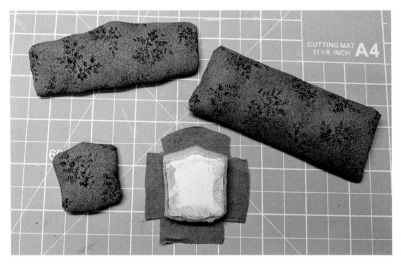

Cut the fabric to cover the cushioning using the previous upholstery as a pattern.

Place the new upholstery in the furniture pieces.

Trim the upholstery with tiny braiding to complete the furniture.

Use the old fabric as a pattern to cut the fabric that will be used to reupholster the furniture. Make sure that the fabric is cut straight and according to the pattern. If the cushioning foam is still intact it can be reused. It is best to cut new cardboard pieces and use the old ones to take the pattern. Once the fabric and cardboard pieces are cut, cover the padded cushioning and back cardboard with the new fabric, and glue it tightly round the cardboard at the back.

The corners and edges must be neat. Before gluing the cushioning back into the frame of the settee be sure they fit precisely in place. Glue the upholstery in place using PVA or craft glue. Use a small damp cloth to remove unwanted glue that would smear on to the fabric. Let the glue settle for a couple of hours.

To add that extra detail, trim the settee and armchairs with 2mm-thick braid. The same method can be used for dining-room chairs and stools.

The Bedding

Whether the bed is a double bed, a single bed or even a child's bed, it is the most important feature in the bedroom. The bedding is eye-catching and gives the room warmth. A standard manufactured bed might definitely need a makeover and an extra touch of detail.

In the Victorian period most bedding was white in colour and made out of linen or cotton trimmed with layers of ruffles and decorated with embroidery, ribbons and fine lace. To make new bedding for the bed, fine linen or cotton in white, ivory or ecru, lace trimmings, ribbon and small braiding will be needed.

IDEAS FOR BEDDING FABRIC

Embroidered cotton lady's handkerchiefs and soft lace doilies can make attractive miniature bedding once they are adapted to fit a dolls' house bed. It is important that the pattern and design suit the project.

The miniature bed before it is given new bedding.

Fabric and lace trimmings that can be used to make the bedding.

The first step when changing the bedding is to gently remove any fabric from the mattress and the bed's frame. Cut a piece of cardboard with the same measurements as the mattress, and place it at the back of the mattress. Cut a piece of white cotton fabric big enough to cover the front and sides of the mattress, with a few centimetres of allowance to cover the back of the mattress. This will be the fitted mattress sheet.

Next cover the mattress with a new piece of white cotton fabric and fold it neatly round the sides towards the back. Glue the white fabric to the cardboard at the back of the mattress and let it dry.

Dismantle the bedding and cut a piece of cotton to cover the mattress.

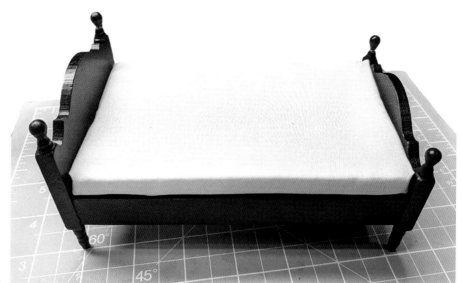

Cover the mattress with a new piece of white cotton fabric and place it on the bed.

	hem allowance	
Length of the floor drop	Size of the mattress	Length of the floor drop
	hem allowance	

Optional lace trimming

hem allowance

hem allowance

Optional lace trimming

Fabric for bedding

How to measure the fabric and lace for the new bedding.

Cut the linen fabric, put up the hems and add lace trimmings for the sides of the bed.

Add the lace on top of the linen cover.

Complete the bed with pillows, cushions and other decorations.

Measure the length and width of the mattress. Depending on the bed's height and design, measure the length of the sides from the top edge of the mattress down to the floor. If the bed has a footboard then there is no need to add the length of the drop at the foot of the bed. With a cast-iron bed the length of the drop at the feet has to be included. The drop for the three sides of the bed must be equal in size, though this is also optional. The length of the sides can be slightly shorter, especially if lace trimming is added.

Depending on the height of the bed, add the measurements accordingly to the two side drops and the foot of the bed if needed to the measurements of the mattress. Add a 1cm (0.4in) allowance all round for the hem. Once the fabric is cut, set the fabric on the bed to check if the measurements are correct; adjust these as required. Fold the 1cm allowance on all the four sides, and neatly hand stitch the hem; alternatively use double-sided adhesive fabric iron-on hem tape so the fabric won't fray, and iron the fabric for a neater finish. At this point the mattress and the three sides of the bed should be covered with the fabric.

Using the same measurements, cover the fabric with lace and layer rows with lace trimmings at the sides of the bed.

Decorate the bed with braiding and tiny bows made out of ribbon. Pillows and cushions can be made in the same fabric trimmed with lace.

Cushions and Pillows

Cushions and pillows are attractive decorations for armchairs and beds. They are fun to make and can

Making cushions and pillows for the dolls' house furniture.

be hand sewn in different shapes and sizes using matching fabric filled with cotton wool. In this book simple square cushions are used to decorate the parlour and the bedroom. The same method can also be used to make pillows. Using the provided template, draw two 3cm (1.2in) squares for cushions and two rectangles 6 by 3.5cm (2.4 by 1.4in) for the bed pillow on the reverse of the front fabric, and cut neatly round them leaving approximately a 5mm (0.2in) seam allowance round the edges.

Hand stitch the two fabric layers together leaving one of the sides open. Trim off the corners of the seam allowance without going too close to the stitching line so the corners remain neat.

Turn the fabric right side out through the opening, and push the corners out using a ballpoint tool. Stuff the cushion cover with cotton wool. Neatly slipstitch together the remaining opening edge of the cushion.

Decorate the cushion with braiding and lace trimmings.

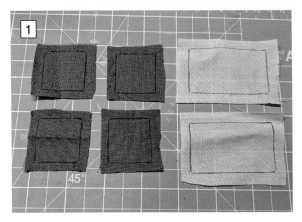

Cut two sets of fabric from the templates provided for each cushion or pillow.

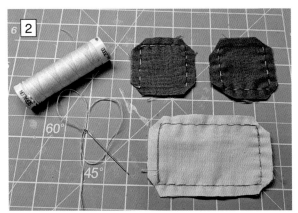

Join the two pieces of the cut fabric together and sew three sides on the reverse.

Turn the fabric inside out, fill the cushions with cotton, and sew the remaining side to close.

Decorate the cushions and pillows with braids and lace trimmings.

Table Runners and Doilies

Table runners and doilies are really easy to make. Table runners can be used on a rectangular dining table, a sideboard and even a dressing table, for which the runner can be made with a double-edged lace trim. Lace trims come in different colours and widths and can be purchased in the length required from haberdasheries and craft shops. Find small detailed designs that will suit the dolls' house, in the width needed for the miniature furniture. Round lace glass coasters make perfect tablecloths for round dining tables.

Doilies were very fashionable during the Victorian period. They were used to protect

Double-edged lace trimmings make great table runners, while lace glass coasters are ideal for round tables.

Adding table runners and doilies to the miniature furniture.

Embroidery flower patches come in different sizes and shapes, and are perfect for dolls' house doilies.

Tea Towels, Dishcloths and Pot Holders

The soft furnishings that can be made for the kitchen in the Victorian dolls' house are quite easy to do, and add to detail when the right type of fabric is used, such as cotton and linen. Using the provided templates will help achieve the right measurements.

In this dolls' house tea towels are displayed folded and hanging. Cut a rectangular piece of linen measuring 6 by 3cm (2.4 by 1.2in). The short edges of the rectangle can be decorated with a piece of lace trimming, attached with a little smear of craft glue. The edges of the linen fabric can be frayed to have a fringe, then a colourful thread hand stitched above the fringe.

Using a toothpick, add a tiny smear of craft glue on the longer edges of the rectangle, and fold 5mm (0.2in) towards the wrong side of the fabric. Fold the tea towel at the middle and hang it anywhere in the kitchen.

furniture surfaces from being scratched by any decorative ornament that was put on top. Tiny lace embroidery flower patches – also found in a haberdashery – make great miniature doilies. These can also be cut out from a lace trimming with a circular or oval pattern within the lace trimming. Doilies can be used in any room around the dolls' house.

Making tea towels, dishcloths and pot holders.

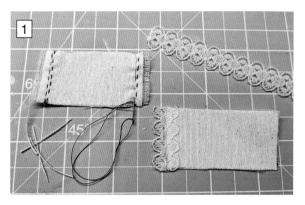

After cutting two pieces of fabric for the tea towels, decorate the edges with lace, or fray the fabric.

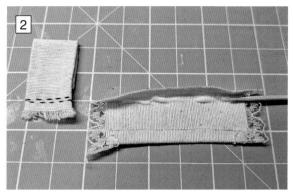

Smear craft glue on the hem of the longer edges, fold the tea towel and hang it up.

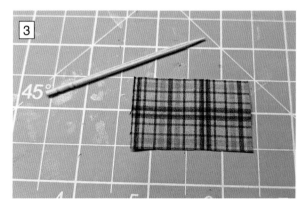

Cut a piece of chequered fabric to make a dishcloth.

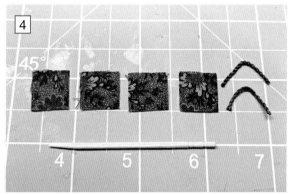

Cut four squares from a decorative piece of fabric and use embroidery thread to make the loops.

Add the embroidery thread to form a loop, and join the two squares together with glue to make a pot holder.

Dishcloths are made with linen or with patterned cotton; a colourful chequered small pattern is ideal. The fabric for the dishcloth should be cut in a rectangular shape measuring 4 by 2.5cm (1.6 by 1in). The edges of the dishcloth can be frayed. It can be displayed folded, or hanging close to the sink.

Pot holders add a nice touch to any kitchen and are very simple to make. Cut four squares of cotton fabric with a pattern measuring approximately 15 by 15mm (0.6 by 0.6in). Add a strand from a cross-stitch cotton thread, turn it to a hoop and glue it to one of the corners of a square on the back side of the fabric.

Smear some PVA glue at the edges of the two fabric squares at the back, and glue them together. Cut the two edges neatly together if necessary. Make a pair of pot holders and hang them from their hoop close to the oven.

Bathroom Towels and Rugs

In the Victorian era towels and bathroom rugs were made out of woven cotton and linen; towels were much smaller and narrower. Use white or ecru-coloured cotton fabric to make towels. Cut the fabric from the template provided in a rectangular shape measuring 8 by 4cm (3 by 1.5in). The edges at the short edge can be decorated with lace trimming

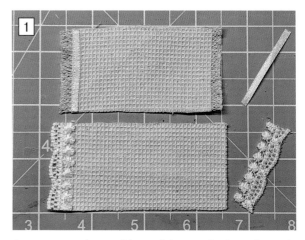

Cut two pieces of cotton fabric and decorate the short edges with lace and ribbon.

Making towels and a rug for the bathroom.

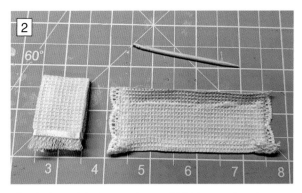

Glue the hem of the longer edges and fold the towels to decorate the bathroom.

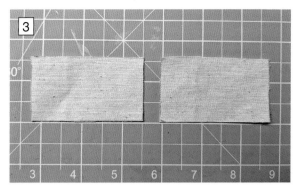

Cut two rectangular pieces of linen to make the bath rug.

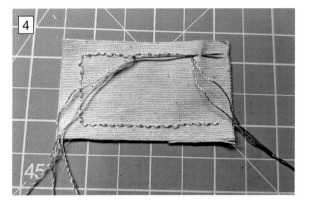

Hand stitch the two pieces of fabric together with a colourful embroidery thread.

Fray the edges of the linen and brush down the fringe to complete the rug.

or a thin silk ribbon. A short fringe can be made by fraying the fabric.

Fold the longer edges of the fabric towards the centre at the back, and secure the edges with a tiny smear of glue. Fold the towels in half and hang them in the bathroom.

Bathroom rugs can be made in any dimension. In this project the rug is made with two rectangular pieces of linen fabric each measuring 7 by 4cm (2.7 by 1.5in).

Using a strand from a colourful cross-stitch thread, neatly hand stitch the sides of the two pieces of fabric together, leaving approximately 5mm (0.2in) allowance. The thread will keep both the

fabric pieces secure and at the same time will add a colourful trimming to the rug.

Fray the four edges of the two pieces of fabric to make a fringe. If necessary cut the fringe so the four edges are neat. Brush down the fringe for a better finish.

Carpets

Carpets and rugs dress up every room of the dolls' house and make it look cosy; they keep homes warm, especially during the winter season. Dolls' house carpets come in various sizes, thicknesses, colours and shapes, and can be purchased from most dolls' house and miniature suppliers. Make sure that the colour scheme and size fit well with the design of the rooms within the dolls' house.

Some small carpets and rugs are easy to make. One such is a small kitchen rug made from jute burlap ribbon, which comes in different widths.

Cut the rug to the desired length. Fray the edges of the ribbon on both of the sides to make a fringe.

Smear a tiny amount of glue at the edge of the rug so the ribbon won't fray more than it should. Brush down the fringe.

Decorate the rug by drawing lines or different designs with colourful marker pens that don't bleed. These rugs can also be decorated with lace and cotton trimmings.

Various miniature carpets that can be purchased from dolls' house suppliers.

Jute ribbon can be found in various sizes. It is ideal for making miniature rugs.

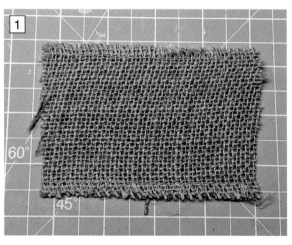

Cut a piece of jute ribbon to make a rug in any size you like.

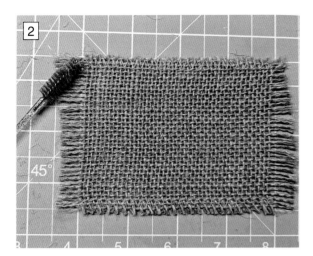

Fray the short edges of the rug and brush down the fringe.

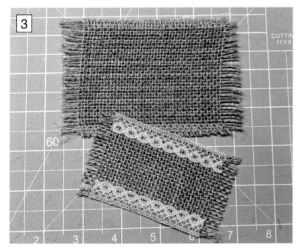

Decorate the rugs with cotton trimmings or with colourful marker pens.

DRAPES AND CURTAINS

The last important soft furnishings to be added to the dolls' house are drapes and curtains. In the Victorian period, rooms had two types of curtain fabric. So-called drapes were made with thick, heavy fabric and hung from massive decorative curtain rods, while lace-frilled netting curtains hung from

smaller rods that were tucked behind the main rod. The curtains behind the windows add a great deal to the décor of the front of the dolls' house. Valances were also added to important rooms such as the sitting room and bedroom.

Readymade miniature drapes and curtains can be purchased from dolls' house suppliers and artisans, but they are quite simple to make. For this project typical Victorian curtain rods will be used.

It is important to know what to measure before cutting the fabric for curtains, especially for the windows used for the dolls' house project. First the width of the window frame needs to be measured to establish the length of the rod that is to be used. Add approximately 2cm (0.8in) on each side of the width of the window frame to determine the length of the curtain rod. The curtain rod must be hung about 1cm (0.4in) above the window frame. Curtain rods that can be adjusted to the required length can be found in wood and in metal from most dolls' house suppliers.

MAKE YOUR OWN CURTAIN RODS

There is an easier way to make your own curtain rods: bamboo skewers cut to the right measurement and two miniature brass door knobs glued at both ends, make great dolls' house curtain rods.

The measurements for the drapes and the curtains depend on how long the rod is and how high it is above the window. First measure the length of the curtain. This in turn depends on the length of the drapes, which in the Victorian period would hang from the rod to the floor. Measure the length from the curtain rod to where the dolls' house floor should be, and add a 2cm (0.8in) hem allowance to both the top and bottom.

The width of the drapes is measured differently, as it must be double the length of the curtain pole for more fullness, whilst also leaving a 2cm (0.8in) hem allowance on each of the sides. Once the fabric

Making curtains and drapes for the dolls' house.

With curtains, windows look dressed up, from both inside and outside the dolls' house.

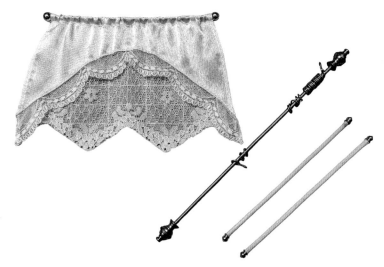

Curtains and rods can be purchased ready made from dolls' house suppliers. Curtain rods can also be made with bamboo skewers and a pair of miniature door knobs.

Measure the curtains to fit the length of the curtain rod for width, and from where it is fixed to the floor for length.

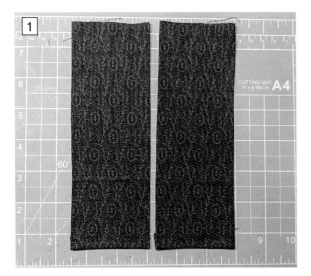

Cut the decorative fabric for the drapes.

Cut the lace for the curtain.

Cut the valance from the decorative fabric and add lace and ribbon trimming to the edge.

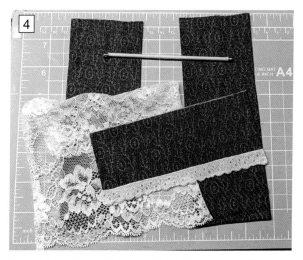

Gather all the pieces of the cut fabric and the curtain rod that is to be used.

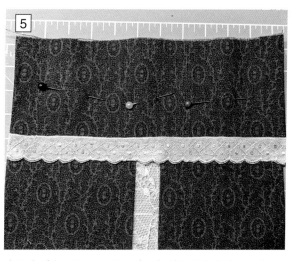

Place the fabric pieces on top of each other, with the lace at the bottom, the drapes in the middle next to each other, and the valance on top.

Hand stitch the curtains, drapes and valance round the curtain rod.

Fix the complete curtains above the window.

is cut, fold it in half and cut the fabric so there will be two equal drapes for each side of the window. Neatly fold 8mm (0.3in) of fabric at the side edges and the bottom hem of the drapes. Instead of hand stitching, a thin fabric iron-on double-sided adhesive hem tape can be used. Once these are ready put them aside.

The lacy net curtain is next. Preferably it must cover the window sill, and always leave a 2cm (0.8in) fabric allowance for the rod. The width of the curtain must also be double the length of the curtain rod, with a 1cm (0.4in) hem allowance on each of the sides. The lace doesn't need to be cut in half like the drapes. Fold the side edges of the curtain and use the adhesive hem tape, depending on the edges of the lace that has been used; put the curtain aside.

For those who would like to add a valance, it is important that its width is double the length of the curtain rod, with a 1cm (0.4in) hem allowance on each of the sides. Leave a 2cm (0.8in) fabric allowance at the top for the curtain rod. Lace or ribbon trimmings can be added to the bottom edge of the valance for more detail.

Once the lace curtain, drapes and valance are completed, they can be hung on the curtain rod. It can be seen that the curtains and drapes are too wide for the curtain rod, but remember they must be gathered at the top to have more fullness.

MAKING PERFECT PLEATS

To have perfect pleats on curtains, drapes and valance, a miniature fabric pleater board can be used. Always remember not to use the pleater board where the fabric has to be folded on the curtain rod. Instead of using fabric starch spray, hairspray can be used to keep the pleats nice and stiff.

Place the two drapes next to each other over the lace curtain, keeping the top edges together. If a valance is to be added as part of the curtain rod, this should be placed over the drapes. These can be pinned together so the edges meet neatly.

Fold the edges over the curtain rod and hand stitch the top edges and the set of curtains tightly underneath the curtain rod with the fabric being gathered. Make sure that the drapes are the same length. The sewn hand stitches must be small to make the gathers for the curtains neat.

Fix the fabric nicely, and tie a piece of lace trimming or silk ribbon to draw the drapes to one side so the lace curtain can be seen. Use tacky wax or craft glue to fix the curtain rods with the curtains and drapes above the window.

Make curtains using the same method but in different designs and fabric for all the windows of the doll's house.

Complete the curtains with tie-backs.

CHAPTER 8

ACCESSORIES FOR THE DOLLS' HOUSE

The dolls' house is almost complete, with the necessities and the furniture pieces all in place. Now all that is needed are the details, and this is achieved through the addition of miniature accessories – and the more detailed the accessories, the more real the dolls' house will look. This doesn't mean that it has to look cluttered – rather, it is more about understanding the perspective of the rooms to make them look more lived in and cosy.

Accessories are tiny objects that can be placed on walls and floors and on furniture. There are thousands of dolls' house accessories available from different periods and in different styles – indeed, the objects and decorations found in a normal house are undoubtedly also available in miniature. They can generally be sourced from dolls' house suppliers and artisan sellers.

A few accessories that will be used for the dolls' house.

An example of a dolls' house room filled with accessories.

DECORATING THE ROOMS

When choosing accessories for a particular dolls' house or room it is important to make sure they are of the right scale and size to fit well. A few miniatures that are slightly bigger or smaller won't give the project that final closure as they should. Style and period are also important, and the miniature accessories should be of the same period as the dolls' house; therefore make sure that those selected for the Victorian dolls' house are not too modern for the period. Having said that, it is quite acceptable to use a few older accessories in a later period – just as in real life, vintage and antique pieces are still found in the modern home.

Collecting miniature accessories can be expensive, and most miniaturists take their time to collect those they need. However, the good thing is that quite a few can be home made, using tiny things found around your own home. All that is needed is some craft material and imagination.

A few supplies that might be found around the house to make your own miniatures.

DECORATING THE HALLWAY

On entering a house, the atmosphere must be welcoming. Even though the hallway is narrow and can't accommodate much furniture, some accessories can still be added. Pictures on the wall will look effective in any part of the hallway, and

The hallway stand decorated with accessories.

picture frames can be found both with pictures and without. Empty picture frames give more opportunities to use your own pictures once these are cut to fit in the frame. A wall clock or a barometer might also be hung on one of the walls. A mirror will look good on a hall table, and table ornaments and a vase with flowers will add some colour.

Miniatures that are found in the hallway.

In the Victorian period a hall stand was a popular feature in a hallway. It was used to keep walking canes, parasols, umbrellas and hats, all of which can be made using craft supplies and tiny objects that are found around the house.

Making Walking Canes

Miniature walking canes are very easy to make. All that is needed are toothpicks, tiny decorative jewellery beads or charms for the headpiece of the walking cane, and acrylic paint. It is important to find the right type and size of beads for the cane. The toothpick should be about 65mm (2.5in) long, though adjust this if necessary. Paint the toothpick with black or brown acrylic paint, and add detail to the cane. Glue the bead to the top of the walking cane and let it dry.

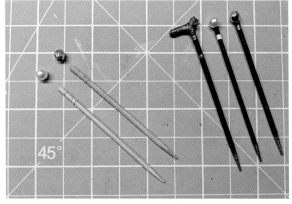

The following items are needed to make walking canes: toothpicks, tiny beads, acrylic paints and glue.

Making Parasols

Parasols were extremely fashionable during the Victorian period, used by ladies during their morning stroll so as not to catch the sun. These are also easy to make. The following items will be needed: a toothpick, a piece of silk fabric, a piece of lace trimming, a small piece of thin ribbon and a tiny bead to put at the head of the parasol.

Using a compass, draw a partial circle on the silk fabric with a radius of 35mm (1.4in), leaving

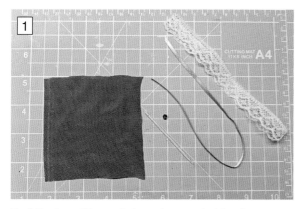

The following will be needed to make parasols: fabric, lace trimmings and ribbon, a tiny bead, a toothpick, acrylic paint and glue.

Cut the fabric in a circle with a radius of 35mm (1.4in), leaving out an angle of 120 degrees.

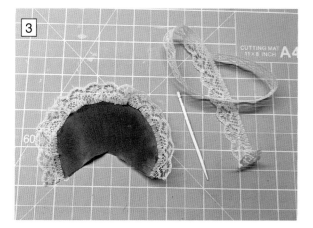

Glue the lace trimming round the circumference of the fabric.

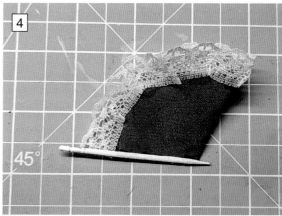

Fold the fabric in half and glue the two joint edges to the toothpick.

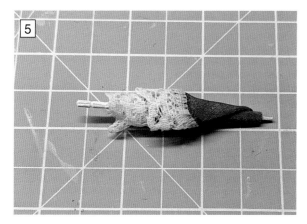

Wrap the fabric round the toothpick and at the end tuck in the corner of the fabric in the folds.

Add a tiny bead at the head of the toothpick and decorate the parasol with ribbon.

out an angle of 120 degrees. Cut the silk fabric accordingly.

Glue the lace trimming round the circumference of the silk fabric. Paint the toothpick in your preferred colour.

Fold the cut piece of fabric and apply a little glue to the toothpick. Glue the toothpick to the straight edge of the folded fabric, leaving the point slightly exposed, and let it set.

Wrap the rest of the fabric round the toothpick and tuck the edge between the folds with a little glue. If necessary, fix the folded lace trimmings to make the parasol look more realistic.

Tie a piece of ribbon round the parasol's centre. Finally glue the tiny bead at its head. It can be decorated with more detail if wanted.

DECORATING THE PARLOUR

The parlour is a room that can take a lot of detail, and beautiful accessories can be used. Because

Accessories that will fit well on the fireplace mantelpiece.

Miniatures that look well on furniture pieces in the parlour.

guests and family gatherings are welcomed in this room, the residing family would decorate this room to show off their wealth and valuables.

Paintings with a gilded frame and large mirrors are essential to decorate the wall, and fit perfectly over the fireplace. A decorative mantel clock can be placed in the centre of the fireplace mantel, with a pair of candlesticks and ornamental figurines on each side. A fire companion and a fire screen will add extra detail to the fireplace.

A tea set with a plate of savouries or biscuits placed on the coffee table will make the room more welcoming for guests. Flower arrangements in vases add colour to the room. Old photos in small picture frames can be placed on furniture pieces, and very effectively fill empty spaces.

Making Books

In the bookcase all sorts of ornaments such as figurines, decorative plates and picture frames can be placed, but generally it will contain mostly books. Miniature books can be purchased in various sizes and colours, but they are simple to make. Thick white cardstock will be needed to make the inner pages, also a scalpel knife, a metal ruler and a home printer.

Book covers can be hand made, or printed on a home printer. Most dolls' house books are about

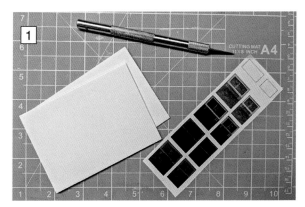

To make books, a scalpel knife, cardstock, book covers and glue will be needed.

Cut out the book covers and the cardstock for the book-page inserts using the templates provided.

Wrap the book covers round the page inserts and glue them in place.

22mm high by 16mm wide (0.9 by 0.6in). Print various book covers in the approximate dimensions. The templates provided at the end of this book can also be used. Cut out the book covers and set them aside. Cut the cardstock in rectangles measuring 20mm by 15mm (0.8 by 0.6in): these will be used for the insert pages of the book.

Books come in different thicknesses, so add cardstock according to the thickness of each book cover. Glue the cardstock to the book cover, and place the books in the bookcase, or on the side table or desk. You can make as many books as you want in different sizes.

The Parlour Bay Window

The bay window can be decorated with a furniture piece and accessories. A chair can fit nicely, or even a small table with a plant in a flower pot.

A small table with a plant in a terracotta pot is placed in the bay window.

To make a simple plant the following will be needed: a leaf paper punch, a small terracotta pot, green leaf paper, putty, glue, and tea from a teabag.

Punch out green paper leaves, shape them, and place them in the putty in the terracotta pot.

After adding glue to the surface of the pot, sprinkle the crushed tea leaves on top.

Highlight the leaves with diluted yellow acrylic paint.

Making Plants in a Flower Pot

Miniature paper plants are easy to make when using leaf-shaped paper punches. These come in different shapes and sizes and can be found in most craft shops. The following items will also be needed to make this accessory: a small terracotta pot, green-coloured paper, a small leaf-shaped paper punch, craft glue, putty, and a teabag.

Punch the green-coloured paper with the leaf-shaped paper punch. Punch as many leaves as will be needed to fit the size of the flower pot being used. Shape the leaves or ferns in a more natural way.

Add a small ball of putty in the flower pot to fit in the punched leaves. Arrange them nicely in the pot. As soon as the leaves are fixed in place add a little craft glue to the pot's surface. Open the teabag and sprinkle the crushed tea leaves on top of the glue; let it dry. The crushed tea looks like compost and soil in the tiny pots.

With a thin paint brush add highlights to the leaves with yellow acrylic paint.

DECORATING THE BREAKFAST ROOM

The dining room, or breakfast room, was one of the most important rooms in Victorian day-to-day life. It was the room where the family shared all their meals, and talked and discussed topics at the table.

The breakfast room can have various kinds of accessory.

It was also the room where most of the necessary chores and preparations were done, such as ironing and folding clothes, sewing, mending and crafts.

This room can be furnished in many ways, and can be changed from time to time. Side tables, wall shelves and small furniture pieces should be decorated with small, useful objects such as are found in a lived-in house. This room might also have been used as a utility room, especially for a middle-class family. Because it was used for purposes other than dining, the miniaturist is offered many possibilities. Picture frames around the walls make an attractive addition, as can a wall clock, which is not difficult to make.

The Dining Table

In this room the dining table holds centre stage. Whatever its size or shape, it is the most prominent piece of furniture in the room and it is therefore important that the way it is decorated makes a statement. Usually this involves setting it for a meal, very often dinner.

There are two ways of decorating the table for the family's meal. Most commonly the dining tableware, cutlery and glasses are set before the food is placed on the table and served. Alternatively the table can be presented with the food already served, with miniature food portions on the plates, and tureens and platters filled with food.

Other ways of decorating the dining table are with craft making, family games, house chores and home schooling.

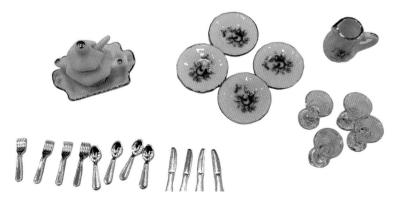

A miniature ceramic dining set and cutlery that will be placed on the dining table.

The table is being prepared for dinner.

An example of a dining room set with crafts.

Making a Wall Clock

To make a wall clock all that is needed is a flat button, a printed clock face and a clear glass dome cabochon.

Fit the clock face in the button and place the glass cabochon on top.

A wall clock can be made with items found in your own home. To start with all that is needed is a flat button with a rim in any colour; ideally it should have a diameter of approximately 25mm (1in).

Print a clock face that fits in the inner part of the button. Paste a little craft glue in the button and add the clock face. A clear, round, glass dome cabochon can be added to the face of the wall clock to make it look more realistic; this can be sourced from a craft shop or haberdashery.

EQUIPPING THE KITCHEN

The kitchen is one of the easiest rooms to decorate in a dolls' house, largely because there are so many miniatures to choose from. Copper pots and pans, utensils and kettles fit perfectly in the Victorian kitchen, especially close to the oven area.

Ceramic mixing bowls, jugs, pitchers, tin-like canisters and cans fit anywhere to fill the empty spaces. As this dolls' house doesn't have a pantry, food supplies, tableware and glassware should be placed on shelves or in a wall cabinet.

Empty glass jars and canisters can be filled with your own spices and herbs. Food preparation will look very effective on the working surface of a cupboard or side table, with dirty tableware placed close by or in the washing sink. Add as much detail as possible to make the kitchen look more realistic.

Copper pots and utensils are placed next to the oven.

Glass wear, tins, canisters and plates set on shelves and around the kitchen.

Making Sacks for Food Supplies

Certain food supplies such as sugar, flour, grains and seeds were distributed in cotton sacks. In the Victorian period the sacks were reused, mostly for towels. These are also easy to make for the dolls' house: all that is needed is some cotton or linen fabric, some thread and a needle, sand, a piece of string and fine markers.

Fold a piece of cotton or linen fabric. Draw a rectangular shape approximately 6 by 5cm (2.4 by 2in) on the folded fabric. One of the short sides of the rectangle must be on the fold of the fabric so

Any food preparation taking place on the work surface in the kitchen will look very effective.

To make sacks the following will be needed: fabric, needle and thread, sand, a piece of string and markers.

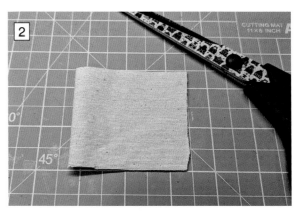

Fold the fabric and cut the three sides leaving a 5mm (0.2in) seam allowance. A template is provided.

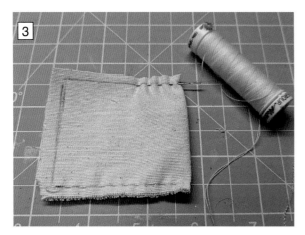

Hand stitch the two edges of the sack together.

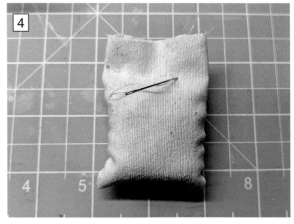

Turn the sack inside out, fill it with sand, and hand stitch the opening of the sack.

Write the ingredients on the sack with markers.

both ends will remain joined. Cut the fabric round the three sides of the rectangle leaving a 5mm (0.2in) seam allowance. It is important not to cut the side where the fabric is folded.

Hand stitch the two long sides of the fabric together.

Turn the sewn fabric inside out and fill three-quarters of the sack with sand. The sand will make the sack look heavy and sturdy. Hand stitch tightly along the top edge of the sack where the sand ends, making sure that the sand stays firm in the sack.

Add a string round the opening of the sack to tighten the top edge close. Write the brand name or

Miniature cleaning tools.

the contents on each sack with a fine marker – black, blue and red markers can be used for this. Sacks came in different sizes so this can be reflected in the dolls' house sacks.

In a small Victorian house the laundry was also done in the kitchen, as the linen and clothes were boiled and scalded on the stove. The iron was also heated on the stove several times while ironing. Thus laundry accessories such as a big pot or even a tin-like washing basin add detail to the kitchen. Cleaning utensils can also be included in the kitchen, such as brooms, mops, buckets, carpet beaters, whisk brooms and dustpans.

Brooms for Sweeping

In the Victorian period brooms were known as besoms and were used both outdoors and around the house. They are simple to make, with a bamboo skewer, sandpaper, glue, string and natural sisal twine rope for the broom bristles.

Cut the bamboo skewer about 8.5cm (3.4in) long. Sand it down to make the broom handle thinner, and remove the polish. Sand down both the ends of the skewer piece to make the edges rounder, like a real broom. The skewer can be stained or painted in a darker shade if preferred.

Cut a piece of natural sisal twine rope and fray the strands as much as possible. A brush and a needlepoint tool will help to separate the strands. Depending how thick the rope is, more pieces might be needed to make the broom bristles fuller.

Gather all the rope strands together and tie one of the ends with a piece of string to keep them firmly together. Cut the end of the broom bristles about 6mm (0.2in) from where the string has been tied to make the strands even. This will be the top part of the broom bristles where the broom stick will fit in. Add craft glue to the top of the broom bristles and add the broom stick in the centre. The broom stick should also reach where the string

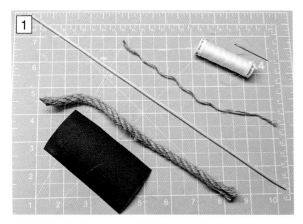

To make a broom the following will be needed: a bamboo skewer, sandpaper, string and jute rope.

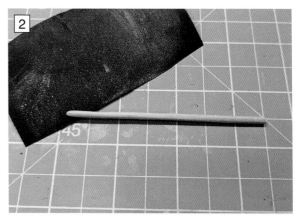

Cut the bamboo skewer and sand it down to make it finer.

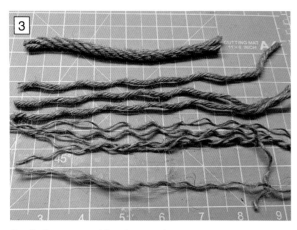

Cut the jute rope and fray the strands.

Tie the strands of the rope with a piece of string and place the cut bamboo skewer in the centre of the tied strands.

Dilute craft glue with water and add it to the bristles of the broom.

Hand stitch the bristles of the broom to flatten it.

has been tied. Let the glue set, and if necessary tie another piece of string round the broom stick and bristles to make it firmer.

A tiny dot of glue round the string can help to keep it in place. Dilute some glue with water, and gently brush down the broom bristles to make them straighter. Don't add too much of the diluted glue to the bristles.

Cut the end of the broom to the desired length. The broom should be about 12cm (4.7in) long. To flatten the broom the broom bristles can be hand stitched at the top, close to where the broom stick and bristles are bound together.

The same method can be used to make miniature whisk brooms and mops.

The same method can be used to create mops and a whisk broom.

DECORATING THE BEDROOM

Apart from the master bedroom, a dolls' house can also have a single bedroom, a children's bedroom and even a servant's chamber. These are decorated differently depending on the size of the room, its style, and the number of furniture pieces that it contains. Less elaborate picture frames and mirrors go well on the walls. If there is a fireplace a pair of candlesticks and a mantel clock would look attractive on the mantelpiece. A fireplace screen placed in front of the fireplace will add detail to the room.

Accessories to be used for the bedroom.

Making the Fireplace Screen

A fireplace screen was essential for all fireplaces, and indeed still is, especially in bedrooms and small rooms. The screen guards against flying embers and sparks from the open fire and prevents unnecessary accidents and fires in the house, and children and pets from getting burnt. It also shields against the intense glare of the light and heat that the logs produce, especially in a confined space.

These screens were quite decorative, and were usually made out of mahogany, glass and brass.

They were also used to display beautiful paintings, stained glass and even needlework. Depending on the size of the fireplace, these screens were made in one or three panels.

A three-panelled fireplace screen will be made for this project, for which the following items will be needed: cardstock, craft glue, gold and brown acrylic paint, a printed picture or piece of fabric for the screen, and fine braiding in a suitable colour. Decorative jewellery embellishments can also be added.

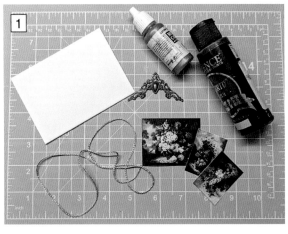

To make a miniature fire screen the following will be needed: cardstock, a picture of your choice, fine braiding, a jewellery piece, glue, and brown and gold acrylic paint.

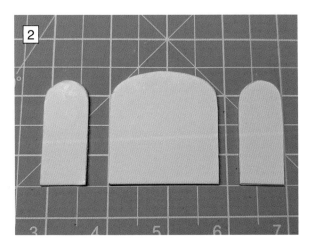

Cut the cardstock using the template provided.

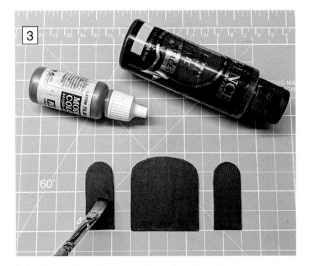

Paint the cardstock brown and the edges in gold.

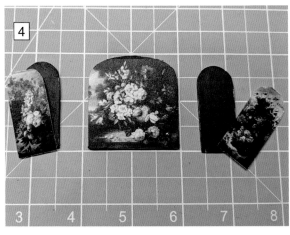

Cut the picture using the templates and glue them to the cardboard.

Add the braiding round the cardstock pieces, except for the bottom part.

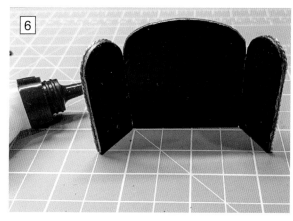

Glue the three parts of the cardstock together.

Add jewellery pieces to the fire screen to add detail.

The finished fire screen.

The fireplace screen will be made out of three rectangles, with the top edge being more rounded. The front panel of the screen must cover the opening of the fireplace. Measure this, and cut the front panel from the cardstock. The two other rectangles should be cut to the same height as the front panel, but they must be narrower – a quarter or a half of the width of the front panel. The template provided in this book can be used.

Paint the three cut panels in brown acrylic paint and the edges of each panel in gold. Let the paint dry.

Use the panels as templates to draw and cut the decorative picture or fabric that will be used for the screen. Glue the cut-out picture or fabric on to the front of each of the three panels.

Trim the edges of the panels with the fine braiding, except for the bottom edge. A bronze colour braid is used for this screen.

Add craft glue to one edge of each of the two narrow panels, and glue them on each side of the front panel at an angle so the screen will stand alone.

For more detail add jewellery embellishments to the screen with a tiny amount of glue.

The fireplace screen is now complete and can be placed in front of the fireplace. This type of screen can be used for any fireplace in the dolls' house.

Bedroom accessories placed round the bedroom.

Toys look very effective in a nursery, as does a water pitcher and basin for a servant's room.

Other Bedroom Accessories

On the bedside table next to the bed a decorative lampshade and a book or two will look realistic, of interest to those who like to read before they sleep. Perfume bottles, a dressing-table set and jewellery pieces are perfect on a dressing table or on a chest of drawers. Garments and clothing can be set on the bed or on a chair. If there is a small desk in the room, more books can be added, a notepad and letters, a quill and inkwell, and a candlestick.

For a children's room, toys and dolls are essential, and for a servant's room a washstand with a basin and pitcher.

DECORATING THE BATHROOM

The bathroom is tiny, but it can still be decorated like any other room. Toiletries are essential. Bars of soap and small bottles can be added to shelves and small vanities. A small wall radiator can be fitted in the room as a heating element. A towel rail with towels can be placed against the wall close to the bath. A pair of small frames can also be added to the walls.

Toiletry and Perfume Bottles

To make toiletry and perfume bottles for the bathroom shelves all that is needed are

Toiletries for the bathroom.

colourful beads in different shapes and sizes. The possibilities are endless: just find the right types of bead to make different types of bottle – basically the beads must be of a good size and able to stand on their own.

Find a tiny bead or jewellery piece to use as a cap for the bottle, and glue it on the top of the bigger bead. For extra detail add tiny labels to the bottles. The same method is used for perfume bottles, which can also be placed in the bedroom.

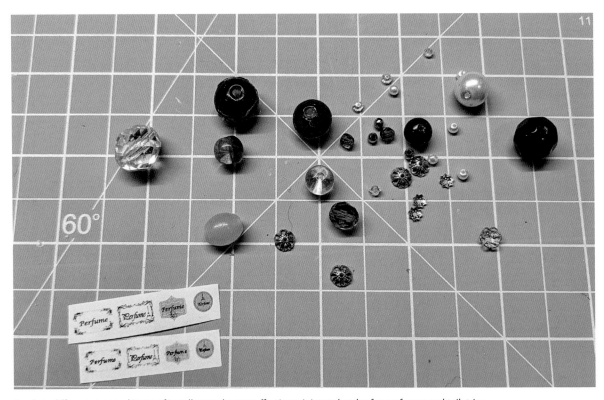

Beads in different sizes and items of jewellery make very effective miniature bottles for perfumes and toiletries.

Glue the beads and jewellery pieces together to make the bottles. Tiny labels can be added for more detail.

CHAPTER 9

COMPLETING THE DOLLS' HOUSE

The interior of the dolls' house might seem to be complete, but rest assured that this is never the case, and further miniature accessories can always be added to your creation.

The interior of the complete dolls' house.

Don't be afraid to move things around: just like a new home being decorated, it is your dolls' house and it can be decorated the way you want it.

Minor additions can also make a difference to the exterior of the dolls' house. It is all about the detail. Take a look at the exterior of a real Victorian house to spot extra detail that might be added. For example, a brass door knocker and a door mail slot are attractive adornments for the exterior door.

Planters with climbers and vines can be added close to the main entrance, and window boxes with flowers placed outside the windows always look attractive. These add colour to the front of the dolls' house.

A real house always has a door number or a name and sometimes even both, giving the building its own authenticity, and a plaque fixed close to the main entrance door adds that extra touch to the front. The dolls' house in this project is called '44, Mornington'. Personalised name plaques can be ordered from a few dolls' house suppliers and miniature artisan artists. Alternatively you can design and print your own. Fix the printed name on some cardstock and add some varnish to seal it.

Sometimes buildings have a street name sign fixed to the façade; this can be added to the dolls' house in the top corner of the ground floor, though choose a name that fits the dolls' house period. Street names can be found from hobby shops, or can be hand made.

Name the dolls' house and attach a plaque next to the main door.

Door furniture such as a door knocker and a door mail slot add detail to the exterior door.

A street name can be added to the dolls' house.

Colourful climbers and windowboxes with flowers add interest to the exterior of the doll's house.

A weather vane and a sundial will add interesting detail to the building.

Dolls and pets might feature as residents in the dolls' house.

A dolls' house room being decorated for Christmas.

A weather vane can be positioned at the top of the roof, and a sundial against the façade: these were very popular during the Victorian period.

One more addition to the dolls' house might be the members of the family, represented by dolls. Be sure they are dressed to match the period of the dolls' house. Dolls can be purchased from all dolls' house suppliers and come in both genders and all ages, and dressed in the style of various periods. Pets might also feature in the dolls' house. Dolls and family pets can give more character to a dolls' house.

Just like a real house, a dolls' house can be decorated for any season and holiday of the year; most commonly this would be for Easter, Halloween and Christmas. Adding a few seasonal decorations will enliven the dolls' house, and after the holiday will give you a purpose to go back and change the décor. Seasonal and holiday accessories can be sourced from dolls' house suppliers and craft shops, and are very easy to make.

DISPLAYING THE DOLL'S HOUSE

Now that the dolls' house is complete it can be carried to the place where it will be displayed: its final destination. Generally a dolls' house is not built in the place where it is going to be displayed in the home. Make sure that it is not set up in direct sunlight or in a humid environment. If it is to sit on a piece of furniture make sure that its base is clean so the surface of the furniture won't be scratched.

Move the dolls' house very carefully. Dolls' houses are often quite heavy, so to avoid damage and/or injury it is best if two people move it; it should also be empty of furniture and accessories until it is in its final position.

As soon as the dolls' house is placed in its final position, connect the lighting strip and the transformer to the electrical house socket. Make sure that all the lighting plugs are fixed in the strip properly, and check that all the dolls' house lights are lit. Now the dolls' house furniture and accessories can be put in place.

Displaying the dolls' house on an attractive piece of furniture.

THE ROOMS IN SUMMARY

The following is a summary of the furnishings and accessories that characterise the rooms in this project dolls' house. Creating these furnishings and accessories has been discussed in the two previous chapters, making every room special in its own way, with its own specific character.

The Hallway
The entrance to the dolls' house is the hallway, which leads to the parlour and has a staircase leading to the first floor. It is small but has a welcoming atmosphere with just the hallstand and a few accessories.

The Parlour
The parlour is a room of refinement, to welcome guests and host special functions. It is furnished

The entrance hallway.

and ornaments. The walls have been decorated with framed pictures and a wall clock. This room leads to the kitchen. In the back wall there is a false door, which gives the illusion that there are other rooms at the back, and a staircase leading to the upper rooms.

The Kitchen

This small Victorian kitchen has a surround for the oven at the back, which is hung with copper kitchen utensils. A side table is set with food preparation and other pantry accessories. Wall shelves with tableware and preserves are positioned above the side table. A small Belfast sink with plates is placed next to the side table. As the room is quite small the wall next to the door is left with a few cleaning accessories.

The parlour.

with Victorian walnut furniture. The upholstery of the settee and armchairs was redone to fit better with the wallpaper and the period. The cabinet is adorned with a collection of books and small ornaments, and the fireplace is decorated with ornaments. The coffee table is laid with an attractive tea-set. A grandfather clock and a small side table were positioned to fill the empty spaces.

The Breakfast Room

The breakfast room is furnished with a mahogany dining table, four chairs and a side table. There is also a small wall shelf that contains everyday objects. The table is set for a meal with a ceramic dinner set and cutlery, and the side table has ceramic tableware

The breakfast room.

The kitchen.

The Bedroom

In the attic the bedroom is furnished with a single mahogany bed dressed with lace and linen bedding. A small combined wardrobe and dresser, together with accessories, is placed against the back wall. In the corner there is a fireplace decorated with accessories and a fire screen. A small desk is placed

The bathroom.

in front of the bed. There is a false door in the back wall that adds depth and detail.

The Bathroom

The bathroom is set next to the bedroom in the attic. It has a traditional Victorian-style bathroom with a claw-foot bath tub, wash basin and chain-pull toilet. A radiator and toiletries are placed round the room. Here, too, is a false door set in the back wall, to match with the bedroom design.

IN CONCLUSION

All dolls' houses are built in the same pattern and manner. Bigger dolls' houses will take longer to build, but the more challenging project is well worth the extra time and effort. Before starting any dolls' house always do some research on the period you intend for your dolls' house.

The bedroom.

Templates for Soft Furnishings

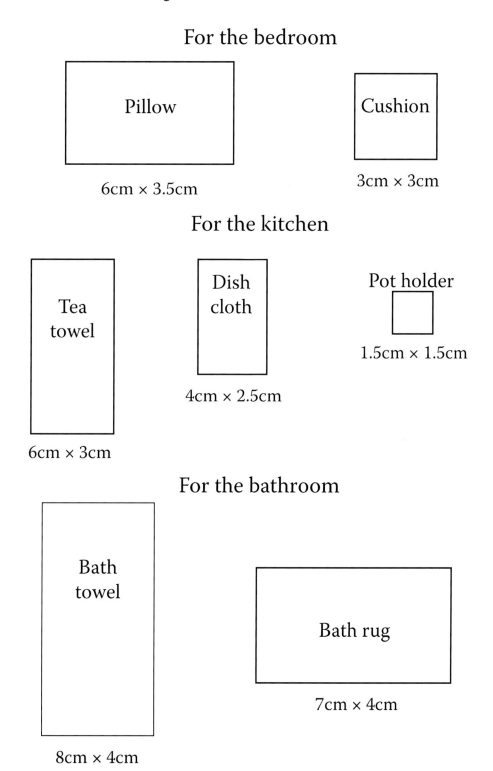

For the bedroom

Pillow

6cm × 3.5cm

Cushion

3cm × 3cm

For the kitchen

Tea towel

6cm × 3cm

Dish cloth

4cm × 2.5cm

Pot holder

1.5cm × 1.5cm

For the bathroom

Bath towel

8cm × 4cm

Bath rug

7cm × 4cm

Templates for Miniature Accessories

Book covers

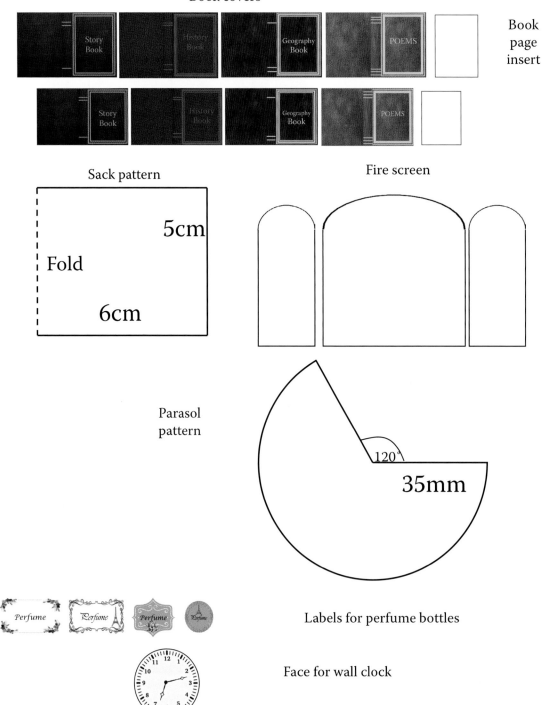

Book page insert

Sack pattern

5cm

Fold

6cm

Fire screen

Parasol pattern

120°

35mm

Labels for perfume bottles

Face for wall clock

SUPPLIERS

For dolls' house furniture, accessories, DIY and lighting:

Bromley Craft Products Ltd
PO Box 283
Uckfield
East Sussex
TN22 9DY
Web: www.craft-products.com
Supplier for textured paint additive and DIY

Dolls' House Emporium
SafeShip House – Unit A
Cullet Drive
Queenborough
Kent
ME11 5JS
Web: www.dollshouse.com

Dolls' House Mania
Grosvenor House
29 Park Lane
Cradley, Halesowen
West Midlands
B63 2QY
Web: www.dollshousemania.co.uk

Hobbies Ltd
Units 8B-11, The Raveningham Centre
Beccles Road
Raveningham
Norwich
Norfolk
NR14 6NU
Web: www.hobbies.co.uk

Melody Jane Dolls' Houses Ltd
Cambrian
Bryn Road
Towyn
Abergele
LL22 9HN
Web: www.melodyjane.com

Minimum World Limited
Unit B, Norfolk House
Sterling Close
Loddon Industrial Estate
Loddon
Norfolk
NR14 6UG
Web: www.minimumworld.com

Stacey's Miniature Masonry
The Workshop
Easthampnett Lane
Chichester
West Sussex
PO18 0JY
Web: www.miniaturebricks.com
For wall bricks and roof tile supplies

Streets Ahead Dollshouse
Unit 6, Bell Park
Bell Close
Newnham Industrial Estate
Plymouth
Devon
PL7 4JH
Web: www.streetsaheaddollshouse.com

INDEX

accessories 6, 10, 17, 20, 44, 50, 56, 63, 64, 74, 82, 84, 85, 90, 114–116, 118, 119, 125, 127, 130, 131, 133, 136, 137, 138
acrylic paint 17, 33, 34, 36, 37, 39–42, 45–48, 60, 76, 90, 91, 116, 117, 120, 126, 129
acrylic varnish 33, 90, 92, 133
alcove 72, 87
allowance 33, 73, 96, 99, 100, 105, 107, 112, 124
aluminium foil 41–43, 45, 46
arm chairs 85, 86, 87, 93, 95, 99, 137
attic 30, 36, 56, 58, 137, 138

bamboo skewers 41–43, 107, 109
bare wood 75, 80, 82, 90
barometer 116
bath tub 88, 89, 138
bathroom 50, 51, 56, 58, 88, 89, 104, 105, 131, 138
bathroom towels 104, 105, 123, 131
battens 40–43
bay window 20, 24, 31–33, 44–47, 56–58, 119
beads 116, 132
bed 87, 88, 95–100, 131, 138
bedding 95, 96, 97, 138
bedroom 13, 50, 56, 58, 65, 87, 88, 95, 100, 107, 127, 128, 130–132, 138
bedside table 87, 131
bookcase 85, 116, 119
books 118, 119, 131, 137
bottles 131, 132
braiding 94, 95, 99, 100, 128, 129
breakfast room 50, 80, 85, 86, 120, 121, 137
brick slips 20, 31–33, 41, 45, 46
bricking 17, 30–33, 40, 41, 44–49
brooms 125, 127
buckets 125
bulbs 63–67, 70
button 122

cabinet 6, 85, 86, 122, 137
candlesticks 64, 118, 127
canisters 122, 123
cardboard 17, 30, 54, 59, 93, 95, 96, 128
cardstock 31, 33, 38, 47, 118, 119, 128, 129, 133
carpet 17, 51, 54, 77, 78, 105, 106, 125
carpet beater 125

carving 17, 18
ceiling cornice 19, 20, 58, 59, 60, 62, 70
ceiling lights 20, 51, 55, 63, 64, 65, 67, 68, 70, 71
ceiling paper 50, 51, 53–55, 76
ceiling rose 69–71
chairs 15, 85, 86, 93, 95, 119, 131, 137
chandelier 63, 64, 68
channels 19, 68, 69, 71
chest of drawers 87, 131
chimney pots 20, 41, 47
chimney stack 20, 36, 37, 40, 42, 43, 47, 48
Christmas 14, 135, 136
cleaning utensils 125
climbers 133, 134
clock 116, 118, 121, 122, 127, 137
coffee table 85, 118, 137
copper tape 63
cotton wool 100
craft glue 17, 27, 31–33, 38, 39, 41, 45, 52–54, 56, 76, 77, 95, 102–104, 113, 120, 122, 125, 126, 128, 129
crafts 121, 122
cupboard 87, 89, 122
curtain rods 107, 113
curtains 17, 47, 107–109, 111–113
cushions 98–100
cutlery 121, 137

damp cloth 27, 45, 47, 49, 95
decorative paper 20, 27, 30, 50–55, 65, 67, 70, 76
desk 85, 88, 119, 131, 138
dining room 50, 56, 58, 65, 85, 89, 95, 120, 122
dining table 86, 101, 121, 122, 137
dishcloth 102, 103
doilies 95, 101, 102
dolls 6, 131, 135, 136
door knobs 20, 56, 80, 81, 91, 92, 107, 109
door knocker 133, 134
door mail slot 133, 134
doors 17, 20, 22–24, 26, 27, 32, 33, 44, 45, 56–58, 80, 81, 91, 92, 133, 134, 137
dormer windows 20, 23, 24, 36–40, 43, 44, 47, 56, 58
double face soft rubber mallet 18, 29
drapes 107, 108, 110–113
drawing room 85
dressing table 87, 101, 131, 137
drill bit 19, 68, 78

drilling 19, 23, 24, 61, 62, 68–70, 78
dry brush 41–43, 45, 47, 48
dry building 16, 25, 26
dustpans 125

embroidered flower patches 102
emulsion paint 17, 27, 30, 34
entrance 11, 50, 56, 57, 75, 84, 85, 133, 137

fabric 17, 90, 92–105, 107, 110–113, 116–118, 123, 124, 128, 129
fabric iron-on hem tape 99, 112
façade 22, 24, 31, 33–35, 45, 55, 56, 58, 133, 136
false doors 80, 81, 138
fibre board 20, 21
figurines 118
fire basket 51, 59, 63, 65, 69, 72
fire companion 118
fire screen 118, 128, 129, 137, 138
fireplace 40, 51, 59, 60, 63, 65, 69, 72, 85, 87, 116, 118, 127–129, 137, 138
floor skirting 19, 20, 58–60, 62, 69, 70, 72
floor tiles 51, 54
floorboard 19, 21, 51, 54
flooring 17, 18, 20, 27, 47, 50, 51, 54, 55, 58, 67, 68, 71, 72, 75, 77
flower pot 119, 120
flowers 85, 116, 133, 134
foam 93, 95
food 87, 121–123, 137
fork prong connector 66, 74
free standing lights 63–65
fret saw 19, 23, 24, 54
fringe 102, 105–107
front panel 27, 33, 35, 36, 38, 55, 56–58, 61, 62
furniture 6, 8, 10–12, 17, 20, 72, 82–95, 99, 101, 102, 114, 115, 118, 119, 121, 127, 134, 136, 137

glass jars 122
glasses 121
glassware 137
grandfather clock 85, 137
grilles 45
grooves 16, 18, 26, 27, 29, 68, 69, 71

hair dryer 53
hall stand 116

hallway 56, 57, 65, 75, 80, 83, 85, 115, 116, 137
hand railing 20, 75–77, 79
hats 85, 116

injury 68, 74, 136

jewellery 92, 116, 128, 129, 131, 132
jugs 122
jute 106, 126

kettles 122
kit 8, 10, 16, 18, 21, 24–26, 29, 55, 65, 69, 75–77, 82
kitchen 50, 51, 56, 58, 59, 65, 87, 92, 102, 103, 106, 122, 123, 125, 137, 138

lace 95–104, 106, 107, 110–113, 116–118
lamp shade 20, 51, 64
landing 20, 23, 75, 77, 84, 85
lead 40, 41
leaves 120
library 89
light wood 83, 84
lights 18, 20, 50, 51, 60, 63–74, 136
living room 10, 14, 50

magnets 20, 61, 62
mahogany 83, 84, 86, 128, 137, 138
markers 106, 107, 123–125
masking tape 16, 26, 29, 44, 45, 71, 73
mattress 96, 97, 99
metal ruler 17, 68, 118
mini saw 19, 59, 60, 77
mirror 85, 87, 116, 118, 127
mitre block 19, 59, 60, 77
mixing bowl 122
mops 125, 127
mortar 31, 33, 41, 45
mouldings 17, 19, 20, 32, 35, 58, 59, 60, 70

newel posts 20, 75–77, 79
notepad and letters 131
nursery 6, 89, 130

oak 76, 83, 84
oven 51, 59, 65, 104, 123, 137

paint brush 17, 31, 33, 34, 36, 38–41, 45, 47, 48, 52–54, 56, 76, 90–92, 120
paintings 118, 128
paper 17, 21, 30, 31, 50, 120
paper punch 120
parasols 85, 116–118
parlour 13, 50, 85, 86, 92, 100, 118, 119, 137, 138
pattern 32, 33, 36, 38, 39, 47, 50–52, 54, 92, 93–95, 102, 103
pavement 24, 47
paving 46–48
pedestal table 85, 87
perfume bottles 131, 132
pets 135, 136

picture frames 116, 118, 121, 127
pictures 47, 115, 116
pillows 98–100
plant 85, 119, 120
plaque 133, 134
plaster 30, 33, 34, 36, 44, 47, 48
plates 118, 121, 123, 137
pleater board 112
pleats 112
pliers 18, 70, 71, 74
plywood 21, 27
pot holders 102–104
pots and pans 122, 123, 125
power rotary tool 18, 68
print 119, 122, 128, 133

quill and ink well 131
quoin bricks 20, 35, 36

radiator 131, 138
rails 19, 20, 23, 59–61
retractable blade knife 17, 26, 33
ribbon 95, 99, 104–106, 110, 112, 113, 116–118
ridge 43, 45, 46
risers 24, 75, 78
roller brush 17, 27, 33–37
roof 17, 20, 23, 31, 36, 38–42, 45, 47, 56, 58
roof tiles 17, 20, 30, 36–39, 41, 43, 45–47
rugs 104–107

sacks 123–125
safety 68, 74
safety glasses 19, 68
sand 34, 123, 124
sand paper 18, 26, 27, 91, 125, 126
sanding down 19, 27, 44, 90, 91, 125
scale 14, 15, 21, 31, 66, 115
scalpel knife 17, 53, 56, 118, 119
scissors 17, 31, 54
scoring 17, 19, 33
scratch built 21, 24
servant's chamber 127, 130
settee 85, 86, 92, 93, 95, 137
shelves 87, 89, 121–123, 131, 137
side cutting pliers 18, 36, 38, 74, 78
side table 85–87, 119, 122, 137
sideboard 85, 101
sink 87, 103, 122, 137
sitting room 50, 56, 57, 64, 85, 107
sketch 21, 25, 64, 67
socket connector strip 20, 63, 65–67, 70, 72–74, 136
soft furnishings 17, 92, 102, 107
spindles 20, 75–77, 79
staining 60, 76, 79, 82, 90, 125
stair rods 77–79
staircase 20, 23, 56–58, 65, 75–80, 84, 85, 137
staircase runner 77–79
stair-rail guard 79, 80
stairs 17, 23, 75, 78, 85
step 75, 76, 78

stove 40, 51, 59, 60, 69, 72, 87, 125
street name 133, 134
string 123–127
study room 89
sundial 134, 136
surround 59, 60, 69

table 85, 86, 101, 116, 119–122, 137
table runner 101
tablecloth 101
tableware 121, 122, 137
tea bag 120
tea set 118
tea towel 92, 102, 103
templates 100, 102, 119, 128, 129
terminal 65, 66, 73, 74
texture paint additive 34
thread 102, 103, 105, 123, 124
threshold 24, 47
toilet 88, 89, 138
toiletries 131, 132, 138
toothpicks 45, 46, 102, 116–118
toys 130, 131
transformer 20, 63, 65–67, 70, 72, 74, 136
treads 75, 76, 77
tureens 121
twine rope 125
two-pin plug 65, 70, 71, 73, 74, 136

undercoat 17, 26–30, 36
upholstery 93, 94, 95, 137
utensils 122, 123, 125, 137

valance 107, 110–113
vanity 89, 131
vase 116, 118
voltage 63, 66, 67

walking canes 85, 116
wall mounted lights 20, 51, 63, 64, 65, 69, 71, 72
wall panelling 19, 51, 60
wall tiles 51, 61
wallpaper 17, 20, 30, 47, 50–56, 58
walnut 83, 84, 86, 137
wardrobe 87, 88, 137
wash basin 88, 89, 125, 138
water 33, 47, 48, 52, 53
water pitcher 122, 130, 131
weather vane 134, 136
weathering 47–49
window boxes 133, 134
window frame 36, 44, 45, 58, 107
windowpane 16, 44, 45
windows 11, 17, 20, 22–24, 26, 27, 36, 44, 45, 47, 48, 56, 58, 107, 108, 112, 113, 133
wiring 16, 18, 19, 60, 65–74
wood glue 17, 27, 33, 37, 57, 58, 60, 77, 82
wood panels 24, 27
wood stain 76, 90
wooden trimming 30, 33, 35, 36, 45, 57, 58

First published in 2024 by
The Crowood Press Ltd
Ramsbury, Marlborough
Wiltshire SN8 2HR

enquiries@crowood.com

www.crowood.com

British Library Cataloguing-in-Publication Data
A catalogue record for this book is available from the
British Library.

ISBN 978 0 7198 4422 5

Dedication
To Matthias, Raquel and Leah.
My very finest and unique creations.
Love,
Mama

Acknowledgements
I would like to thank my husband Gilbert and my children
Matthias, Raquel and Leah for all their love and support
in everything that I do. This book was important to you as
much as it was to me and I wouldn't have done it without
you. Thank you to my devoted parents for their constant
encouragement and for believing in me. You never gave
up on me and my dreams. Thank you my sweet Penny for
your loyalty and companionship throughout the progress
of this book and dolls' house project. Thank you to my
family and friends for cheering me on when I needed it.
Last but not least I want to thank The Crowood Press for
giving me the opportunity and entrusting me to write this
book, and helping me in each step of the way.

Rebecca

Typeset by Simon and Sons
Cover design by Sergey Tsvetkov
Printed and bound in India by Thomson Press India Ltd